808.3
Am3a

64852

DATE DUE

Oct 13 '81

GAYLORD M-2

PRINTED IN U.S.A.

WITHDRAWN
L. R. COLLEGE LIBRARY

AESTHETICS OF THE NOVEL

AESTHETICS OF THE NOVEL

By

VAN METER AMES

Instructor in Philosophy at the University of Cincinnati

CARL A. RUDISILL LIBRARY
LENOIR RHYNE COLLEGE

GORDIAN PRESS, INC.
NEW YORK
1966

Originally Published 1928
Reprinted 1966 by Gordian Press, Inc.

Library of Congress Catalog Card No. 66-29460

808.3
Am3a

64852

February, 1969

Printed in U.S.A. by
EDWARDS BROTHERS, INC.
Ann Arbor, Michigan

TO

MY MOTHER

ACKNOWLEDGMENTS

I am grateful to four philosophers of the University of Chicago: Mr. Moore, who introduced me to philosophy; Mr. Tufts, who taught me aesthetics; Mr. Mead, who inspired my book; and Mr. Ames, who inspired me.

I wish also to express my gratitude to the Graduate School of the University of Cincinnati for generous assistance in the publication of the book.

V. M. A.

CONTENTS

I

WHY WE ADMIRE ATHLETES

Our first problem is to keep on our feet, to keep going. In the most sedentary occupation the essential thing in life is to be physically ready and fit. If a man have not the strength to sit up and take nourishment, if he cannot hang to a strap on the way downtown, if he cannot sit at his desk throughout the morning, he cannot tend to business. He must first tend to himself. The most sublimated life rests upon a physical substructure, and the more lofty a life becomes the more solid should be its basement. Primitive buildings and their denizens kept to the earth. Early men were not tempted to neglect their physical basis when it was their whole life. Among animals hardly anything but physical fitness counts, and in so far as men are animals it is the same with them.

Among boys the more alert and agile are the leaders almost solely on account of their athletic ability. The prestige of athletes continues and even increases through high school and college, partly due to the organization and propaganda of athletics, but chiefly to the prime importance of the physical in life. The popular heroes in the world of grown men are athletes. Prize fighters come first, because, more than wrestlers or swimmers or runners, they exhibit all-around physical perfection; they are trained to what is still regarded as the manly art; and they do not, like team athletes, rely on the help of others. For five hundred thousand years survival has depended upon physical qualities, and while civilization has brought new values, it has not changed the fact that the first condition of existence in a physical world is a physique. Our greatest concern is for health, as shown by our forms of greeting to each other as well as by our sympathy for the sick. We like children to acquire intellectual and social graces, but first we want them to be well and strong. Next to having healthy children, we like to have hale old people. We wish children to be physically prepared for life, and we like to see old people who have not been broken by it. In all stages of life, as well as at the beginning and at the end, health is the sign of fitness. By association health comes to be regarded as a good in itself, even when it goes beyond fitness, when it really ceases to be health, as in the case of athletes whose bodies have become maladapted to real life. Most people, however, not being strong enough, are refreshed by the sight of superabundant strength in their athletic fellows as well as in the nudes of Michelangelo.

Almost as much as excessive strength, exceptional skill in useless performances is admired by relatively awkward, unco-ordinated people. Health is so precious and precarious, and we are so sensitive about our physical selves, that whatever our success in business or society we are humiliated to play a clumsy game of golf as much as to be found wanting on the scales. Man remains a schoolboy in that, however wise or great he may become, physical *gaucherie* makes him feel more ridiculous than any other kind of left-handedness. A boy's aptitude for mathematics or for music may compensate for lack of athletic ability, as a man's wisdom or eminence may compensate, but it is often poor compensation.

The delight of the intellectual Greeks in beautiful bodies showed their recognition of this basic fact of life, that "no matter how elaborate or how 'lofty' the pursuit in which we are engaged, it involves throughout accommodations of the organism."[1] The Romans also knew the necessity of a sound body for a sane mind, but they did not know the moderation of the Greeks. Instead of enjoying the harmonious development of the Olympic athlete they gloated on the brutal strength of the gladiator, thus helping to bring about the Christian denial of the body, which in turn gave way to the exuberance of the Renaissance, and the athleticism of today.

The emphasis in modern education upon sport is inherited from the efforts of Italian schoolmasters of the Renaissance to give their pupils Grecian bodies as well as Greek and Latin learning. But we have carried it to such an extreme that our educational institutions are largely advertised by and attended for their athletics, while the efficiency of the methods and instructors in that department excels all the others. The value of physical culture is obvious; but to abdicate the cult of intelligence and become exclusively devoted to that of the muscles is dangerous. The lure of sports may be due to the fact that people who indulge in physical exer-

[1] Elizabeth Kemper Adams, *The Aesthetic Experience,* p. 47.

cise to the neglect of intellectual exercise are likely to be light-hearted, handsome, and gay, and much better company than those who think too much. Certain it is that those whose higher brain centers are overtaxed by modern life are inevitably refreshed by regarding the reposed faces and glowing bodies of swimmers who spend their days in the sun and water, of happy children, and island races who live like children.

Marcel Prévost reminds us that the division of mankind into two categories, the intellectual and the muscular, is artificial and recent: "Sophocles was a complete man, athlete and poet. So, too, were Marcus Aurelius, Montaigne, and Goethe. Any number of modern artists and savants are intellectuals accustomed to all the exercises of the body."[2] The fact remains, however, that the first requisite in society, in the movies, in the novel—everywhere except perhaps in the correspondence school—is a good physical presence. Other qualities may enhance it or make up for its lack, but none may take its place. This is most evident in sex attraction, though perhaps the woof of all human relations is dyed with sex. It may be objected that physique is no more important sexually than intellect or spirit. It has been said, for instance, that in the lists of love the consumptive poet will carry the day against the athlete. The explanation may be that the poet's pitiful want of the health the other has calls out a stronger response in the form of sympathy. The truth is after all that the poet's attraction is physical quite as much as the athlete's, though it is inverted, while in addition he has the

[2] *L'Art d'apprendre,* pp. 161 ff.

charm of his imagination. Then, too, if intellect were of first importance the athlete should have an easy victory, because his undeveloped mind would be so pitiful in his glorious body that any generous-minded lass would feel far greater compassion for it than for the undeveloped body of the poet. But no one wastes charity on the ignorant athlete; everyone's heart goes out to the pale poet; *ergo,* muscle is preferred to mind. Hence why is not any gibbering wreck of humanity on a par with the poet in our sympathies? The reason is that the poet is exquisitely aware of what he lacks, singing of heroes and gods and angels, apotheosizing the body that is his torment. We see that were not the golden tide of life miserably denied him he would be an Olympian, whereas the bum in the gutter would at best be only an athlete. But what is an Olympian but a super-athlete? It is because the poet is finally thought of as a better athlete than any athlete that we admire him.

By thus taking the extremes of muscular and mental perfection and comparing their appeal we are able to see which part it is in the "complete man," athlete or poet, that is more valued. But why is man more vain of his animal body than of his human mind? It is because for five thousand years he has been building cities and civilization, while for five hundred thousand years he has been building a body for life in the open. His habitat is unpaved nature: for that he is fitted, and that alone can exercise his inherited capacities to satisfaction.

We love nature because she is the best trainer of athletes. She first developed them and she best can keep them fit. Our faculties are adjusted to her exercises, our eyes to her sights, our ears to her sounds, our legs to her distances. We are like children kept in school, like animals kept in cages, eager to get out in the race-remembered scenes with their familiar surprises. We yearn for the forests, the waters, the mountains.

We are surprised that Benvenuto Cellini made no mention in his *Memoirs* of scenic beauty on his trip through Switzerland, that Petrarch was the first man to climb a mountain for pleasure. Yet we today, with all our love of nature, are almost lacking in appreciation of arctic scenery. That is because man has never abundantly adapted himself to the arctic, that part of nature being most beautiful to him which has most often been his home, though inasmuch as he can live almost anywhere, almost any spot may appear beautiful to him. Uninhabitable spaces, however, are likely to be sublime or awful rather than beautiful, on account of their inhospitality to man. The Alps were not attractive to Cellini because he thought of them merely as being in his way on his journey to the court of France. Their snowy glare was not beautiful to Stevenson because, hemmed among them for his health, he regarded them as prison walls. Mountains are now attractive to leisured persons with surplus energy as offering a glorious opportunity for exercise; but before Petrarch mountaineering was merely a disagreeable adjunct of war, inconceivable as a pastime save for the gods on Olympus. As for Olympus, the Greeks did not wish to live there themselves, but imagined for the souls of their virtuous dead the flat Elysian Fields. We, however, whose lives are flat, are lifted up by the grandeur of the mountains, from whose Pisgah heights all the surrounding country looks like the Promised Land.

Leonardo was the first to paint a landscape; but he was surely not the first to love one. No one can read Homer's "Hymn to the Earth" or St. Francis' "Hymn to the Sun" and deny in them the love of nature. If this sentiment is more common now it is because man has been separated from his mother, Nature, and misses her in town. He goes to see her in the country; he brings her into the city and walks with her in the park; he paints her and writes to her; he longs for her even in aspects which he had not appreciated before, as Stevenson has shown in his essay on the enjoyment of unpleasant places. In short, all nature has become beautiful. We like the hills because they are high, the prairies because they are wide, the storm because it is bracing, the calm because it is soothing. To make a poem a poet has only to describe nature, tell where he saw her and how she was arrayed: verse and rhyme are not necessary, for if he write in prose with feeling, his words will surge like the Mississippi through the forest, and rhyming poets will come to him for inspiration, as they came to Chateaubriand.

The most fascinating part of all nature is the sea, because it is the source of life. We have washed up from the sea, and like waves on the beach are drawn back. We like the land, for there we were brought up; we love the ocean, for there we were born. We have never been weaned from water; every cell in our bodies must be bathed in it or die. Wheresoever we wander we must take water with us; we look for it in oases, pray for it in dew or rain, and kneel to it in rivers like Gideon's men; we beautify our gardens with it and build our summer homes beside it. Nothing is more vivifying than a plunge in it, as Thetis knew when she dipped her baby in the Styx. A stream is a blessing; an ocean is ineffable. One who cannot go to it should read Conrad's *Mirror of the Sea,* Loti's *Pêcheur d'Islande,* Dana's *Two Years before the Mast,* Melville's *Moby Dick.* The sea, like the mountains, is a challenge to us, to the viking in us; it contains mysterious monsters; it is the route to exotic lands and luxuries; and from its wide horizons our homes acquire the quiet charm of havens. But the real reason why men have been entranced by sea stories from Homer to Conrad is an unconscious nostalgia for the cradle of their being. Swinburne has expressed this feeling for the sea in his "Ballade of Swimming":

BALLADE OF SWIMMING

The sea is awake, and the sound of the song of the joy of her waking is rolled
From afar to the star that recedes from anear to the wastes of the wild wide shore.
Her call is a trumpet compelling us homeward: if dawn in her east be acold,
From the sea shall we crave not her grace to rekindle the life that it kindled before,
Her breath to requicken, her bosom to rock us, her kisses to bless as of yore?
For the wind, with his wings half open, at pause in the sky, neither fettered nor free,
Leans waveward and flutters the ripple of laughter; and fain would the twain of us be

Where lightly the wave yearns forward from under the curve of the deep dawn's dome,
And full of the morning and fired with the pride of the glory thereof and the glee,
Strike out from the shore as the heart in us bids and beseeches, athirst for the foam.

Life holds not an hour that is better to live in: the past is a tale that is told,
The future a sun-flecked shadow, alive and asleep, with a blessing in store.
As we give us again to the waters, the rapture of limbs that the waters enfold
Is less than the rapture of spirit whereby, though the burden it quits were sore,
Our souls and the bodies they wield at their will are absorbed in the life they adore—
In the life that endures no burden, and bows not the forehead, and bends not the knee—
In the life everlasting of earth and of heaven, in the laws that atone and agree,
In the measureless music of things, in the fervor of forces that rest or that roam,
That cross and return and reissue, as I after you and as you after me
Strike out from the shore as the heart in us bids and beseeches, athirst for the foam.

For, albeit he were less than the least of them, haply the heart of a man may be bold
To rejoice in the word of the sea as a mother's that saith to the son she bore,
Child, was not the life in thee mine, and my spirit the breath in thy lips from of old?
Have I let not thy weakness exult in my strength, and thy foolishness learn of my lore?

Have I helped not or healed not thine anguish, or made not the might of thy gladness more?
And surely his heart should answer, The light of the love of my life is in thee.
She is fairer than earth, and the sun is not fairer, the wind is not blither than she:
From my youth hath she shown me the joy of her bays that I crossed, of her cliffs that I clomb,
Till now that the twain of us here, in desire of the dawn and in trust of the sea,
Strike out from the shore as the heart in us bids and beseeches, athirst for the foam.

ENVOY

Friend, earth is a harbor of refuge for winter, a covert whereunder to flee
When day is the vassal of night, and the strength of the hosts of her mightier than he;
But here is the presence adored of me, here my desire is at rest and at home.
There are cliffs to be climbed upon land, there are ways to be trodden and ridden: but we
Strike out from the shore as the heart in us bids and beseeches, athirst for the foam.

While landscapes and sea scenes are beautiful because of their vital relation to us, the heavens and heavenly bodies are inseparable from the terrestrial setting, and the sun is of especial importance to us, having warmed life into being in the ocean and sustained it on the land. Juanita Miller, the daughter of Joaquin Miller, was formally married to the sun in July, 1923, but all things that live are wedded to him. Darkness is death and has ever shrouded lurking death. Fire was first sought because, like the celestial lights, it dispelled darkness, and like water it is so vital to us that it has become a symbol for life itself.

We are drawn to nature through our inherited adaptation to her, and we admire athletes because they are close to nature. Our interest in them is not disinterested. We like them because they are fit, but also because the sight of them makes us fitter, as we reverence the saints not only for their holiness but for the redemption of our own lives through their example. "Can a man help imitating that with which he holds reverential converse?" asks Plato. Almost we can gain salvation by imitating animals and athletes. The relaxation of a tiger, the sleep of a lion, the stretching of a cat, the ease of a swimmer, the effortlessness of a runner, the grace of a dancer are all akin to the serenity of a saint in resting and refreshing us, soothing and reassuring us, toning our tired nerves, restoring our very life.

II

WE ADMIRE ART FOR THE SAME REASON

We admire art for the same reason that we admire nature and athletes, namely, that it refreshes us. Man, like a stringed instrument, has an organization or structure capable of various responses when played upon, some of which express his nature more than others.[1] Those impressions which arouse in him the vibrations most congenial to his being are invested with the pleasure felt and called beautiful. The studies of the Germans in *Einfühlung* or empathy have shown that pleasure in audition and vision is largely due to unconscious accompaniments of breathing and balancing. Some sights and sounds impede, others facilitate, these accompaniments, and that is the reason why "some shapes (independent of what they represent) are liked and called beautiful and other shapes disliked and called ugly. . . . . This is the essence of beauty—the possession of a quality which excites the human organism to functioning harmonious with its own nature."[2]

This quality of beauty is possessed twice over by the open spaces of the world, its waters, woods, and mountains; first, because there the air is sweet to the lungs and the opportunities for bodily movements are obviously manifold; second, because there pleasant shapes

[1] Lipps, *Ästhetik*, I, 9.

[2] E. D. Puffer, *The Psychology of Beauty*, p. 15.

and forms are found in profusion. Yet the landscape gardener may heighten even the beauty of nature by selecting and rearranging her most delightful characters. Whereas in nature the effects are often confused or scattered, in the garden they may be composed and bounded. Its plan controls the eyes to movements of accommodation which are pleasantly accompanied by the deep adjustments of respiration and equilibrium; while its boundaries limit the eyes to a space they can compass without fatigue, bringing them back again and again to the fascination of the arrangement, which is both stimulating and relaxing, because free and yet determined.

The beauty of what we see, whether in a garden or in a building or in a statue, is not in what we see, but in what the vision makes us feel. On the canvas there is nothing but juxtaposition of colors: the work of art is in the mind. What the artist puts into the object is only the preliminary foundation of the work of art. What the hewn marble is aside from the apperception of the observer is never an object of our feeling and fancy; only our scientific thought may examine that.[3] It is through an ellipsis that the physical things which are mere aids for the reproduction of the beautiful come to be thought of as themselves beautiful.[4]

Then the question arises why we attach aesthetic pleasure to objects. The answer is to be found in the functional relation of the aesthetic attitude to experience as a whole. The customary view is that this attitude has no application beyond itself. Logically and historically,

[3] Volkelt, *System der Ästhetik,* chap. i.

[4] Croce, *Estetica,* p. 107.

however, aesthetic values always appear within problems. Without problems they would not exist, because aesthetic values are cues for responding to a problematic situation. Our conduct is always in adjustment, and hence we are constantly (if unconsciously) on the lookout for the cues or values which from the affective standpoint enable us to act. Even the surprises of life indicate that it is a constant anticipation of the unexpected. We all have to adopt the "peculiar rocking, swaying motion" of Rikki-Tikki-Tavi. "It looks very funny, but it is so perfectly balanced a gait that you can fly off from it at any angle you please."[5] Were life static or comatose, were routine and habit unbroken, we should not have aesthetic thrills. They come when we are in doubt, in difficulty, in the moment when a solution flashes upon us. A suggestion of the way out, a message of coming relief, a glimpse of solace, a promise of deliverance—that is the nature of the aesthetic experience.

It is the moment when Fatima, on her knees beneath Bluebeard's scimitar, hears her sister Anne call from the tower of the castle that there is a cloud on the horizon, approaching swiftly—a band of horsemen—her brothers coming to save her! It is the last minute of play, the fourth down, with the score tied, when the quarterback skirts safely around the end, while the interference picks off the intervening tacklers, stunned by the thunder from the grandstand. It is when the crowd of accusers have dropped their stones and left the woman alone with the Master, and he says unto her, "Neither do I condemn thee: go, and sin no more." It

[5] Kipling, *The Jungle Book,* p. 190.

is in the quiet of the cathedral, of the study, or the garden, in the moment of insight, when "the loud vociferations of the street" are hushed, when the strain is relieved and we gather strength. Or it may come in the street itself, when we are most intent upon our business, as it came to Paul on the road to Damascus.

The mystical vision is the supreme form of the aesthetic experience, the contemplation of the highest possible values, those answering to the problem of the universe itself. Not only is the mystical experience aesthetic, but every aesthetic experience is mystical to some degree. It is always an escape from the pressure of earthly existence to a communion with the ideal. Beauty never exists as other things do, never quite comes down to the common level, though it may subsist in certain situations as their essence, their meaning. Though brought forth on the earth, it is fathered by a god; an aura of divinity hovers about it; flowers spring up in its path; men feel faint with exaltation at the sight; they think of heaven and their short life seems worth while. Like Helen, beauty draws all eyes to itself, filling them with wonder; but no more than Helen can it be successfully espoused and possessed. When the attempt is rashly made it recedes like a phantom, for though all men are subject to beauty, it is subject to none of them. It does not reside in objects, though it transfigures them upon occasion, because it is our way of looking at them that makes them look beautiful to us. When a problem, like an upward flaw, forces things out of their obscurity into a new light we see them as if for the first time and are transfixed; yet if we reach out to take them their beauty vanishes like a colored bubble, leaving nothing behind but the pipe and suds from which it formed. The *Non Toccare* of the art museums must be the motto of all seekers after beauty. It is not enough to handle it with care; we must not touch it; hardly may we breathe in its presence.

But while the aesthetic experience often occurs spontaneously, as if sponsored from heaven, it may be induced by art. The essence of intelligence is to control nature, to find the conditions of pleasant experiences in order that they may be repeated at pleasure. It is not intelligent to leave the most valuable things to chance when forethought would insure their appearance whenever desired. Men naturally have ideas under certain circumstances, but the circumstances are not certain without educational institutions. Men are naturally religious in some moods, but those moods are not regular without churches. Men are naturally industrious under the pressure of necessity, but their industry is not dependable without organization. Indeed, there is nothing natural to men which does not gain in security and dignity through intelligence, and the sense of beauty is no exception.

To become intelligent about the aesthetic sense we must discover the conditions under which we are aware of it, ascertain its place and its function in our lives. Does it belong to the stream of immediate, habitual experience which flows along without the control of consciousness? or does it inhere in a problematic situation which habit is unable to meet without the help of active attention and reflection? Inasmuch as aestheticians are agreed that the aesthetic attitude is not passive but active, that it involves consciousness and even self-consciousness in a conspicuous degree, it must belong to the problematic rather than to the unproblematic sphere of life. Consciousness, active attention and awareness, do not appear except when summoned by the breakdown of the automatism of habit, and habit does not break down unless confronted by a novel juncture that is too much for it. If the aesthetic experience requires consciousness it can occur only within a problematic situation, for there only does consciousness occur. But within that situation, as Mr. Dewey has analyzed it, there are several stages, and the question is which one of them is the locus of the aesthetic experience. There is first the interruption of habitual activity with the initial awareness of difficulty, perhaps no more than a sense of uneasiness; then comes contemplation of the situation, during which cues for response to it, suggestions of solutions, emanate from it; then comes the elaboration of these suggestions and their formation into a hypothesis; and finally the verification of the hypothesis. (Mr. Dewey does insert another step after the first interruption of unconscious habit, in which he says the difficulty is defined and clarified, but he admits that this step is often omitted, and that suggestions begin coming before the trouble has been analyzed very far.) Now the aesthetic experience, while it is one of active attention, is not strictly one of reflection, of ratiocination. Hence it must come between the stage of the felt difficulty and the stage of reflection. It is the first contemplation of the elements in the situation which are the cues for response to it, its values, before a hypothesis is formed or a solution attempted.

The aesthetic attitude is located where the flow of habitual activity has been checked by a problematic situation, in the lull before reflection sets in, while the values are being contemplated for their own sake. This attitude arises, however fleetingly, whenever a problematic situation is confronted. But such a situation may be created deliberately for the sake of the aesthetic attitude involved in it, may be planned and refined by the means of art just for the sake of aesthetic enjoyment. Art is the artifice for checking the unheeding march of habit and drawing us up short before the values of a problem, objectifying them in such a way as to facilitate our attention to them and enhance our pleasure in them. An artificial aesthetic effect is as breath-taking as any; it, too, seems to descend from the cerulean, for the more intelligently it is planned the more unsought and unavoidable it will appear.

The aesthetic experience being the contemplation of value, it will be well to consider what value is. It is not purely objective and not purely subjective. It is, as Heyde has shown, a relation of an object to a subject, involving pleasure and a certain depth of feeling.[6] But why that relation should subsist, why it should involve pleasure and depth of feeling, is the important question. The answer seems ready enough if we approach it in terms of a problematic situation. Values are the data, the elements in such a situation, which serve as cues for

[6] Johannes Erich Heyde, *Wert (Eine Philosophische Grundlegung)*, Erfurt: Verlag Kurt Stenger, 1926.

the solution of it; they appear only in that setting and they persist until the solution is reached. The real ground of value is a problem. If the problem is a lasting one, so is its corresponding value; if it is a universal one, so is its value; if it is local or transitory, even so its value. Apart from a problem of some sort, there could be no value of any sort. The value of food corresponds to the problem of satisfying hunger; the value of a bridge corresponds to the problem of crossing a river; the value of a friend corresponds to the need of friendship; the value of a stove corresponds to the want of warmth. And the contemplation of every value is in itself aesthetic. But when one passes beyond contemplation of it for its own sake to reflection upon how to attain it and the actual effort to achieve it, one passes beyond the aesthetic stage. What the artist does is to objectify and fix values in such a way that our attention to them just for themselves is facilitated. We may go on to think about them and to try to consummate them, but that is not his affair primarily; that is outside the frame of his picture, beyond the close of his novel.

The artist does much more than represent values; he also presents them. His picture may represent love. But it also presents color, light, line, and shade, which are not represented but actually present values to us. They delight the eye, and through their composition and harmony compose and harmonize our entire being. These values in a picture depend considerably upon the nature of our organism, its past experience and its present state, whether its need is to be soothed or excited. Yet in so far as its needs are constant, those works of art which minister to them will have constant value. Whatever our surface mood, our basic nature remains fairly homogeneous, so that whatever works may attract our passing fancy, there are some which will retain our abiding affection.

Values are as complex as we are. Food may look good to us because we are hungry, but it may also appeal to our craving for color, and it may be so shaped and arranged as to satisfy our demand for form and pattern. A bridge, too, besides its evident value for crossing the river, may absorb our admiration by the curve and contour of its lines and surfaces. The stove, also, besides being aesthetically attractive as such, if we are cold, may take on charm through its design. And finally, our friend himself, besides being a joy to us just as a friend, may bring joy to us in other ways: through the grace of his figure or the timbre of his voice. These additional values are just as real as the others, and often more so, for they may remain even when we are not hungry, have no desire to cross the river, warm ourselves, or see our friend; for balance and harmony in the form, shape, and pattern of things are of constant value to a bilateral being who looks through two eyes, breathes with two lungs, stands on two legs; and we are so made that color, sound, taste, smell, and touch have a valuable effect upon us, in connection with other values or independently of them, when they stimulate us to responses harmonious with our nature.

Values, to remain aesthetic, must be contemplated for their own sake. This requires leisure and release from the pressure of the very problems which engender them; otherwise we find ourselves hurried past the beautiful moment into reflection, and swept thence back into action. Then, too, we must learn to seek the values we need, and not merely wait for them to turn up. We must go to nature, where we know that our hurried habitual life will have to slow down and absorb beauty. We must go to the art museums where the works of the artists will stop and hold us for a space in the ideal world. We must learn from the artists to see beauty everywhere, to burn always with Pater's hard, gemlike flame. As he says, in a sense our failure in life is to form habits: "for, after all, habit is relative to a stereotyped world, and meantime it is only the roughness of the eye that makes any two persons, things, situations, seem alike. . . . . Not to discriminate every moment some passionate attitude in those about us, ... is, on this short day of frost and sun, to sleep before evening."[7]

For the sake of the world's work it is well that most of us do some sleeping before evening, for to him who has been awake to beauty it is sleeping to work, to carry out plans and pursue a purpose, because all this involves a program and regular habits through which we must leave beauty's side. The worker, the enterpriser, the go-getter cannot maintain the attitude of an observer, an aesthete, a Marcel Proust. The world as will and action is not the world as idea and contemplation. To live the life of will is to sleep, because this existence knows not itself nor aught else: it just is.

There is, however, no absolute break between aesthetic and other experience. The effect of beauty does

[7] Walter Pater, Conclusion to *The Renaissance*.

not evaporate when one gets home from a concert or finishes reading a novel, and there are on-and-off beats in the busiest day, so that a man may intermittently contemplate that which he loves, as a clerk may glance at the picture in the lid of his watch. No gang is worked so relentlessly that it may not stop now and then to light a pipe and gaze up at the sky; no office force is forbidden to look out of the window once in a while, or to look inwardly upon an invisible horizon. The mystics say that however brief their vision, the memory of it's sweetness never leaves them. Through an instant one may behold eternity, as through a knothole one may see high heaven, and a lifetime would not be long enough to forget it.

Indeed, the aesthetic experience can exist at all only as a phase within non-aesthetic experience. It consists in the contemplation of values, and values answer to problems. Thus if a person could escape into an ideal existence, such as Santayana suggests,[8] where there were no problems to be dealt with, his leisure could not be filled with the enjoyment of the infinity of art, as Santayana imagines, for art, the representation of values which arise only in problematic situations, could mean nothing to him. To live such a life, more surely than to indulge in unmitigated work and endeavor, would be to sleep before evening. There would be no art in a realm of pure art, just as there would be no idea in a world of pure idea. The aesthetic attitude very soon palls and disappears when abstracted from its logical and functional place as a phase in the response to a problematic

[8] *The Sense of Beauty*, p. 30.

situation. The mystics, who contemplated the highest conceivable beauty, found that they could achieve the ecstasy of direct insight into it only occasionally, and that they never could maintain it. Nearly all of them ceased trying and turned to founding orders or building hospitals, discovering that through seeking problems rather than through avoiding them they could live closer to their beautiful ideal. It is also the experience of everyone that beauty plucked from the living situation which brings it forth is a faded thing, and for that reason it is often fresher and more genuine outside museums, where it arises naturally and unsought. Vernon Lee speaks of vainly going again and again to the galleries in Florence in search of the aesthetic thrill, until one day, exhausted, she abandoned the attempt and dropped down on a bench in the Baptistery to read a newspaper. Happening to glance up, her attention was caught by the swirl pattern on the floor, and she was enthralled by its beauty. That is to say that beauty, like pleasure, to be got must be forgot.

Pleasure accompanies the termination of desire in its appropriate object, and aesthetic pleasure is no exception. It accompanies the envisagement of the values in a situation which first of all is problematic. It is when our alertness for cues enabling us to cope with that problem is rewarded by their appearance that we experience aesthetic pleasure. It is the moment when the solution is foreshadowed, when our striving has not ceased, but is poised and calmed by the contemplation of its consummation. Striving and straining alone are not aesthetic, nor is consummation; but the blending of the two constitutes the aesthetic experience. This is the stimulation in repose which aestheticians are always talking about. That phrase takes on real meaning when interpreted in the light of a problematic situation. There is no striving, no effort, no expansion or expression except through the stimulus of a problem; and there is no rest or respite to our effort, no limit to our expansion, no form or shape to our expression, except in contemplating the solution of the problem. This is the vital relation of expression and form in art. Expression in itself is not really expression, it is just a push, a gush; form in itself is not form, it is just a dead stop, a standstill. They become themselves when they come together to make beauty, and they come together at the moment when the blind drive of the organism under the stimulus of a problem becomes conscious of the solution, when it thereby comes to a pause, a balance; the moment when the wild plunging and thrusting of impulse is checked and directed by reason, harmonized and tranquilized; the moment when instinct becomes insight; when the *frein vital* of Mr. Babbitt is applied to the *élan vital* of M. Bergson.[9]

We may justify Croce in saying that beauty is nothing but form, and that form is nothing but expression. A blind response to a problem becomes true expression only when it is harmonized and balanced, *formed*, through contemplation of the outcome: that is to say that expression and form are the same thing, and what else is beauty? Beauty is the control of spontaneous response by an end or purpose. It is freedom in necessity, as Kant said. Beauty always strikes us as fresh

[9] Irving Babbitt, *The New Laokoön*, p. 212.

and free, and at the same time as inevitable. Its freshness is due to the uniqueness of a problematic situation; its inevitableness to the necessity of dealing with a certain problem in a certain way. The solution of each problem is something novel, but it is always determined by the factors in that problem, and cannot be other than it is. The response to each problem is initially free in the sense that it is haphazard and undirected; it becomes determined by reason at the moment of insight into the elements of the situation. Beauty is the union of the unconscious response pushed by the problem behind with the conscious response controlled by the solution ahead. It is the mergence of Schopenhauer's world as will with his world as idea—the will still strives, but its striving is controlled. As Hegel said, desires are mitigated and passion relieved when brought before man as idea. The beautiful moment comes when the end is envisaged, when the values are discerned which will be consummated in the outcome; and the beautiful moment lasts as long as these values continue to be contemplated and enjoyed for their own sake, before any move is made toward the dénouement which they point to. It is the moment when we at last see before us what we long for, before we have got to it, when we are arrested by the sight of it at the same time that we are drawn on by it. Art is the artifice for representing this moment; but this moment is beautiful whether we come on it with or without the aid of art.

The experience of beauty is the most intense and poignant that we have, combining the immediacy of impulse and the vividness of feeling with the clarity and comprehension of reason; here we feel and know at the same time that the meaning of life is before us. It is all there, the effort, the conflict, and also the end of the effort, the resolution of the conflict. Here is what we have sought; our quest is finished, and we are filled with joy; but no! the end is not yet; we cannot stop here, and our joy is steeped in sorrow, for the lovely moment cannot stay. By its own momentum it is carried beyond itself, and that too is a part of life, all of which is focused in that magic, tragic moment. Just when we seem to have attained beauty we realize that it is unattainable. It smiles wistfully upon us and fades from us at the same time. That is why those who are most sensitive to beauty are more happy and more sad than other folk. They know that beauty is both a joy and a sorrow forever.[10]

The aesthetic moment is the contemplation of value, and value is the projection of our need, our want, our lack. Hence the pleasure and the double pain. What pleases us is the presence of what we desire, but what pains us is that it is not truly present, or we should not desire it, and what pains us further is that were it to become really present it would be more than ever absent, since then we could not even contemplate it at a distance. Value signifies a wish, and when the wish is fulfilled the value vanishes.

The function of art is to enable us to recall the moment of beauty. In the work of art we may ever again perceive the will becoming idea, the opposing forces be-

[10] Motto of Giordano Bruno, quoted by Schopenhauer in *Die Welt als Wille und Vorstellung:* "In tristitia hilaris, in hilaritate tristis."

ing reconciled, the discords being harmonized, again feel stimulation in repose, again be soothed and saddened. The difference between the real and the false work of art, or between the good and the bad, is simply that the former repeatedly brings back beauty like Aladdin's lamp, whereas the latter becomes impotent to do so. A work which stirs us more than it is able to still us may thrill us once like a detective story which keeps us up half the night, but it cannot do it again, because its method is too crude and obvious. It is like a toboggan-slide which one climbs up just to coast down: it takes too long to work up and the let-down is too fast to please a mature mind except in its puerile moods. It does not bring about stimulation in repose, but stimulation and then a drop. That is the nature of excitement, of dissipation, but is not the essential nature of art. A detective story is not even exciting more than once, for after one reading the consummatory aspect consumes the rest of it, and it becomes as stale as ashes. Mr. Dewey says, "The 'eternal' quality of great art is its renewed instrumentality for further consummatory experiences."[11] That is to say that great art is always able to reinduce a state of vital relation between active yearning for an end and calm contemplation of that end.

This point indicates that values are active as well as passive. As passive they are projected by problems; as active, they in turn project problems. A problem sets up its own solution as an end; and an end also sets up the problem of its own attainment. If a man is thirsty, he wants water; and if he sees water it may make him

[11] *Experience and Nature*, p. 365.

thirsty. If a man has a deep urge to distinguish himself he will set up a high ideal as his end; and if a high ideal is held up before him it will make him ambitious to distinguish himself. Now since art is the representation of values, it, like them, is both passive and active. In relation to the artist it is passive, it is a record of the artist's aesthetic experience; but in relation to the audience it is active, it tends to produce in them the experience which the artist had; it tends to put them into the midst of a problematic situation at the aesthetic phase, the point of balance between scattered centrifugal responses going off in all directions, and concentrated centripetal control. When art is successful this is exactly what it does; when it is unsuccessful this is just what it fails to do.

Of course, to be successful a work of art must be applied to a susceptible subject; just as a drink of water to be appreciated must be proffered to one who is a bit thirsty, whether he be aware of his condition beforehand or not. But artistic taste may be cultivated to the same degree that sensitiveness to problems may be educated. The richer our experience of life, the richer our appreciation of both life and art; and the deeper our acquaintance with art, the deeper our understanding of both art and life. Progress in life is in the direction of enriching perceptual content and deepening conceptual control, and it is not different in art. In their eulogistic sense life is artistic and art is lifelike. What is most important in both is the aesthetic phase of a problematic situation, the moment when divergent impulses are reconciled by reason, when instincts are transformed by intelligence, when formless, meaningless movements take on form and meaning, when the various elements in a situation become unified in a pattern or design, when the parts are ordered into a whole, and the many become the one.

The initial diffuseness of the responses to a problematic situation is not yet art, and their final fusion is beyond art. Art is their first fusion, when the sparkling contact is just being made between the two opposite poles of experience, the initial or the instrumental phase of a problem, and the final or consummatory. In art there is a reciprocal relation between means and end, there is an interpenetration of instrumentality and consummation. As Mr. Dewey says, false theories separate these and restrict art to consummation, thereby setting it apart from other experience, whereas it is rather a perfection and purification of the aesthetic phase of all experience.[12] That is the tendency of classicism, to exalt the final stage when effort has eventuated in the end term, and to disparage the initial and intermediary stages: it reserves appreciation to a privileged aristocracy who take no part in production and are thereby deprived of real appreciation; while it confines creation to a despised, enslaved class who have no share in the significance of their labor, and are thereby made uncreative and mechanical. On the other hand, the tendency of romanticism is to exaggerate the first phase of a problematic situation, the unrestrained release of imagination which has no end in view, the feeling that any end is intolerable, the emotion which is impatient of any

[12] *Experience and Nature,* chap. ix.

controlling or confining form, which rushes skyward to blow the lid off the universe, if there be one. The classic ideal is to lodge in a glorified Hotel Terminus forever, enjoying the completion of a journey that one never took; the romantic ideal is to travel third-class forever, on a trip that will never end. The classic ideal tends toward the serenity of senescence and the coolness of the tomb; the romantic, toward the fever of adolescence and the broken heart of hopeless love. These lines by Goethe illustrate the one:

> Über allen Gipfeln
> Ist Ruh,
> In allen Wipfeln
> Spürest du
> Kaum einen Hauch;
> Die Vögelein schweigen im Walde.
> Warte nur! balde
> Ruhest du auch.

These by De Musset illustrate the other:

> Rien ne nous rend si grands qu'une grande douleur—
> Les plus désespérés sont les chants les plus beaux,
> Et j'en sais d'immortels qui sont de purs sanglots.

Yet classic art, if it is *art,* is not completely classic, nor is the romantic entirely romantic. There is the warmth of "expression" in the quotation from Goethe, and there is the calm of "form" in that from De Musset, else neither would be beautiful. Thus art cannot successfully be divided into romantic and classic: the only basic distinction is between good art and bad art.[13] In

[13] Mr. Dewey points out that there is no separation between useful art and fine or final art, since art is a peculiar interpenetration of means

good art longing and consummation are made one; in bad art they are not. Anatole France said that there are just two things in life—love and death. It is the same in art, but they must *both* be there!

The aesthetic moment is a philosophic pause in which we see them both, and see them as reciprocal, the particularity of desire and the universality of desirelessness. In a real work of art the two are inextricable: the passionate parts fill in the whole, and the dispassionate whole fills out the parts. The parts would not be what they are apart from the complete composition, which in turn would not be itself without its components. The longing and yearning are for the end, and the end is the end yearned for. Neither has any significance without the other, but together they constitute the meaning of art, which is that of life itself: the synthesis of love and death, personal and impersonal, temporal and eternal, private and general, subjective and objective, motion and rest, emotion and reason, instinct and intelligence, particular and universal, perception and conception. In art and life these pairs are reciprocal, for, as Kant said, percepts without concepts are blind, and concepts without percepts are empty, just as women without men are helpless, and men without women are hopeless. To separate the two aspects of a complete work of art is as unhappy as to segregate the two sexes in a complete life.

It is erroneous to say that women are more aesthetic than men. They are more emotional, intuitional, impul-

---

and ends. "Art is the sole alternative to luck; and divorce from each other of the meaning and value of instrumentalities and ends is the essence of luck" *(Experience and Nature,* p. 372).

sive, subjective, and personal; they think in more vivid and intimate terms, are more conscious of the contents of the moment with its shades and shadows, more likely to notice the speaker's tie and the shape of his nose, the style of the furniture and the color of the rug; but all this does not make them more aesthetic than men, for without the complementary masculine characteristics they are not more than half aesthetic. Men are less directly aware of immediate meaning; they are more conceptual; they condense and telescope the data of experience so that they may handle a myriad of them without perceiving any of them. If women are too perceptual, so that it is hard for them to abstract and generalize, like Juliet's old nurse, who could faithfully recall the minutest circumstance in her experience, with all its associations, and could go back and forth along an endless chain of "ands," but who could not jump to a general statement, men, on the contrary, are prone to overlook particulars and forget them, failing to see the trees in the forest. But men as such are not therefore less aesthetic than women as such, but like them, they are halfway aesthetic. The completely aesthetic is a synthesis of perception and conception, of personal and impersonal, of feminine and masculine; it is a wedding of the two. The more opposed these two are, the more they stand in need of being united. Masculine women and effeminate men may be fairly self-sufficient, but womanly women and manly men are naturally drawn together. The work of art *par excellence* is the marriage of man and woman, these twain being the personification of the twin aspects of art.

Philosophers especially need feminine society since they are the most conceptual, that is the most masculine, of men! It is fundamentally unphilosophical to cleave too closely to abstract philosophy, for true philosophy is an artistic harmony of the abstract and the concrete, the universal and the particular; it includes the wisdom of personal love as well as the love of impersonal wisdom. The most serious advances in philosophic thought result from comparatively direct contemplation of the facts; and to the male all facts are female. Pure abstraction is as far from real philosophy as the purely concrete. Schopenhauer says that abstract conceptions are only the husks and shells of thought, that they are characteristic of talent rather than of genius, which always sees the universal in the particular. Genius lives on fresh nourishment from the source of all knowledge, intuition or direct contemplation, whence everything appears to it in lively images and figures.[14] "But," says Bertrand Russell, "the outcome has to be expressed in words if it is to be communicable. Those who have a relatively direct vision of facts are often incapable of translating their vision into words, while those who possess words have usually lost the vision. It is partly for this reason that the highest philosophical capacity is so rare: it requires a combination of vision with abstract words which is hard to achieve, and too quickly lost in the few who have for a moment achieved it."[15] That is to say that philosophy is a subtle synthesis of the dual

[14] *Die Welt als Wille und Vorstellung,* Drittes Buch, Kapitel 31.

[15] *The Analysis of Mind,* p. 212.

aspects of art, and that, like all art, it is subject to deflection and difficult of achievement.

It must be remembered that aesthetic experience is a phase within non-aesthetic experience, that the beautiful moment comes in the midst of other moments as a red-letter day appears among ordinary days on the calendar, and that, like a holiday, it is an interruption of routine by an uncommon occasion demanding special observance. As long as life runs along in the ruts of habit the significance in the world about us is ignored, the poetry in words themselves is overlooked, as well as the sermons in stones. Ordinarily persons, as well as other objects, modestly serve to stimulate the appropriate behavior in us without calling any attention to themselves. We habitually put on our clothes without thinking anything about them, go down the stairs without noticing them, speak to people without seeing them, answer them without hearing them, eat our breakfast without tasting it, read the paper without heeding it, ride downtown without feeling it, and we may move about all day in a familiar world responding and reacting as automatically and unconsciously as a baby in his cradle. We never wake up and really open our eyes and ears unless roused by a difficulty requiring our active attention. On the other hand, we can hardly close our eyes unless circumstances allow us some respite, and, since one puzzle is no sooner solved than others appear, there is really no rest until the final rest. We are always asleep to some things and awake to others, for if attention is attracted to something it is thereby distracted from something else. The analysis of experience into successive phases following in single file is too simple to fit the fact that different orders of experience march abreast. One is at the same time conscious of some things and unconscious of others. In the same step one issues from one maze and enters another. For years one may remain at the aesthetic stage of several questions and be safely arrived at the ultimate station in several others. Every mystery broached draws up the curtain in a new theater of values, every one solved drops a final curtain upon a last act. There are secret places all about us which will reveal their treasures when we are initiated. There are sealed books which will open at the appointed time, sphinxes which will speak when we are ready to listen. Meanwhile we are too busy to be aware of their existence; we plod along in blinders intent upon our errands, or we gaze aside on other charms. Our way is long and its diversions various; every turn in the road opens a new vista, every caravansary for the night brings novel entertainment. But wherever we are, whenever our attention is absorbed by something for its own sake, we experience the aesthetic thrill.

The things which we take for granted, habitually and unconsciously, are not aesthetic. To become so they must appear within the spotlight of a problematic situation and hold the stage; or they must themselves be theaters of such situations, that is, they may be works of art. Anything may accidentally become aesthetic by appearing at a psychological *crux criticorum,* but art is not accidental or adventitious. It is a premeditated, deliberate challenge to habit and routine. A genuine work of art stands always ready to represent dramatically a problematic situation; it actually gives a continuous performance of the drama of life itself, the perennial problem play with the ever fascinating plot of love in death, of stimulation in repose. Beauty is either natural or artistic. Beauty may be produced naturally by a problematic situation, or artificially by the representation of such a situation, that is, by art. But however it be produced, the beautiful is that which delights in itself because it holds within its frame the whole of life, love, and death. Everything is there, the beginning and the end, the finite and the infinite, the bond and the free, conation and cognition, instinct and insight, mystery and revelation, triumph and defeat, hope and hopelessness, all joy and all sorrow. We find ourselves within a work of art, and all our world as well. In art is what we are ever looking for everywhere. Hence its power over us. We can hardly put it down; we can hardly look away from it; and it is impossible to forget it, for it is the very flower of life, and the whole of life, in its complexity and its simplicity. To look upon beauty is in one moment to live, to love, to die. There is nothing left to wait for or to pray for. In one instant of beauty we drink the elixir of all experience; in one heart-beat we live forever and cease to live at all. We are rapt beyond life and beyond death in an unendurable ecstasy which is also a peace above understanding.

Beauty is the mystic rose of the universe, seen by Plato, Plotinus, Dante, and the saints, but also glimpsed, however dimly or inadequately, by every human soul who has ever indulged in drink or drug, or sought and fought and longed, and felt the thrill of love. It is not only the Grand Mystics who have had the mystical experience, for every aesthetic experience is mystical and everyone has aesthetic experience, it being an inevitable stage in the response to every problem, and life itself being one prolonged problem made up of minor ones at every step. The aesthetic moment is mystical because it mirrors the secret of life, disclosing its inner nature, the continual process of Becoming through the melting together of being and not-being. It reveals the there in the here, the then in the now, the future in the present, shows the end implicit in the beginning, the arriving implied in the striving, the fulfillment foreshadowed in the wish, the consummation involved in the aspiration. In the aesthetic moment we see the solution of a problem before we have solved it; we eat our cake before we have had it; we cross our bridges before we have come to them; we leap beyond life before we have lived it. The aesthetic experience includes the mildest anticipation of the outcome of any course of action, as well as the wildest day-dreaming, and the contemplation of genuine art gives this experience of satisfaction in expectancy, of finding in seeking, of tranquility in excitement, of patience in impatience, of rest in restlessness, in which the distinction is dissolved between unattained and attained, possible and actual, unreal and real. This intoxicating state of consummation in aspiration, of security in insecurity, of sanity in insanity, is natural in the response to a problematic situation or in the representation of one by art; but it may also be induced by drugs. Those who are neither innocent nor intelligent enough continually to encounter beauty in the daily course of work and play, enjoyment of nature, companionship of friends, and appreciation of art, seek it in dissipation and indulgence. To the philosopher men are much alike and their aesthetic moments comparable, whether they be inebriated with whiskey, enraptured by a rose by the roadside, absorbed and "lost" in their work, enthralled by a cause, drunk with glory, moved by music, architecture, sculpture, painting, dancing, acting, or poetry, sunk in study, exalted before an altar, overcome by love, or intoxicated by contemplation of the attributes of God, like Spinoza.

In the aesthetic experience we become conscious of the reciprocity of aspiration and consummation, whether it be produced naturally by a problematic situation, artificially by a drug, or artfully by a work of art. A work of art is any work which represents the aesthetic synthesis of stimulation and repose, whether it be a couplet or an epic, a window or a cathedral, a prayer or a religion, a thought or a philosophy, a single action or a whole life. Art includes everything which is arranged or fashioned. The word comes from the Latin *ars* or *artis*, originally "skill in joining or fitting," from the Greek ἄρειν, "to join, to fit together." It therefore includes street cars and ice wagons as well as symposiums and symphonies.

This is not saying that all art is the same, for some is good and some is bad. It is not saying that we should enjoy the contemplation of an ice wagon as much as that of a painting, for a painting may present us with more values and more vital ones. A perfect ice wagon would be just as much a work of art as a perfect picture, but it would be less appealing, because it would answer primarily to a relatively unimportant problem, that of hauling ice. It may be objected that a wagon would haul ice just as well if it were roughly thrown together, with uneven edges and bent-over nails; but then it would not be so economically and nicely adapted to its purpose, and that is to say that it would not be so artistic. Often more art, i.e., more skill and care, goes into making pictures than into making wagons, but not always by any means. Indeed, it is safe to say that the majority of wagons are better works of art than the majority of pictures. A wagon so loosely built that it collapsed in the street, or so stiffly fitted together that it would not move, would publicly disgrace its maker, whereas an equally loose or static picture might escape censure, might even be praised, so much more muddled are people about pictures than about wagons. A picture may always cohere by means of its frame, and it may always borrow stimulus from its association with the magical name of Art; but a wagon must hold together and move by the art that is actually in it.

Art is a fitting together, an adjusting of means to ends, to cope with a problematic situation. There will be as many kinds of art, then, as there are problems, and all of them may be good or bad. The automobile answers to the problem of getting about in town or country. It may be said that then it should be shaped like an oil drop to offer the least resistance to the air. This would be true if its purpose were merely speed; but that is only part of it, along with comfort and commodiousness and safety. Automobiles which are built solely for speed are different. It may be objected that the design and finish of a car has nothing to do with its function; but it really has everything to do with it. The designer must constantly keep in mind that it is an automobile which he is making, and not a ship or a sewing machine. A new design may seem odd at first, but it ceases to seem so if it is really suitable; on the other hand a design begins to look odd as soon as more suitable ones supersede it, though of course fashion, which is adventitious to art, does tend to vitiate taste at this point.

Another thing which enters into the purpose for which an automobile is constructed is the purse of the purchaser, and this must be considered just as much as the other requirements of the machine. A Ford answers beautifully to the need of many people for whom a Rolls Royce would be no solution at all. But still a Rolls Royce is more beautiful? Other things equal it is—assuming that one could afford it, one would prefer it. But other things, namely purses, are not equal, and for those who cannot afford a Rolls Royce it is no help at all, its cost being an insuperable defect. Yet in so far as one may disregard this fault and overlook one's own circumstances, taking the point of view of those more favorably situated, for whom the cost is no part of the problem, it is natural to think that the Rolls Royce is more beautiful than the Ford. This logic, however, does not allow one to conclude that the Ford as such is ugly, for one has only to consider that compared to a magic carpet, which is no more impossible for most people than a Rolls Royce, the Rolls Royce itself is a Ford. This is the sort of reflection which has always led the unworldly to discount the glories of this world, finding true beauty only in the ideal, which alone can satisfy the yearning of the soul.

This is the truth of the teaching that fine art strives to represent the ideal and make it shine through objects of sense. Otherwise it is nothing but snobbery on the part of painting or any other department of art to arrogate to itself the title of Art, or Fine Art, and lord it over the other works of intelligence and skill, calling them industrial, instrumental, mechanical, vulgar. This class distinction in art is often based on a class distinction in society, Art with a capital A being the art which is monopolized by Society with a capital S, stored in its palaces, mansions, and museums. This tends to make essential to art the qualities of costliness and scarcity which are only accidental to it, and to identify art with unsharable goods. The commonest domestic utensils may become objects of art by becoming rare and antique. Even rare copies of them will be accepted as art, but will cease to be so as soon as they become common, though none but a connoisseur could tell the difference, and he only by certain esoteric indexes which may have nothing to do with finish and perfection, that is, with art. Of course there is a genuine and legitimate interest in what is rare, and there is no reason why this should not contribute to the interest of art; but it should not be allowed to constitute art, though it may well constitute a hobby. Every man should have a hobby, and that of antiquarianism is as honorable and as absorbing as any; but the antiquarian as such is not an aesthetician, and his absorption in antique art may lead him to think that it alone is art. Special knowledge regarding the dates and makers of art objects is not the same as appreciation of art itself, though it may very well be conducive to it. A man who knows the true qualities of any art should thereby be helped to recognize them in any other art, but a connoisseur of art is different from one who is merely a connoisseur about art. The one who really knows art will not rank a reproduction below the original unless he can show that it is inferior. And were that reproduction copied a million times he would still appraise and appreciate the last copy in the same way as the first. Those who really love books are not the bibliophiles, whose passion is rather for manuscripts and autographed first editions than for books. This passion is partly the selfish desire for possessing something not shared by others, and partly the superstition that physical and spiritual contact are the same, that what has been touched by a man has thereby been magically charged with his personality. But the only one who truly possesses an object of art is the one who appreciates it, and he alone comes in contact with its author.

The one who really knows and loves art does not classify and rank its works according to fashion, scarcity, costliness, or the number of physical removes from the artist, but solely according to the depth of the aesthetic experience which he enjoys in their presence. The only distinction which he makes in art is between good and bad. Good art succeeds in synthesizing aspiration and consummation, stimulation and repose; bad art fails to do so. If a copy succeeds in doing this it is just as good art as any. The objection is made that copies are mechanical; but they are no more so than the original. All art is mechanical in so far as it is accomplished by means of any sort of tool or instrument. A pencil or a brush is a machine as much as a rotary press, and there is no reason why an artist should not employ a big, complicated machine as well as a small, simple one if it gets good results. Often the results of large-scale production are bad, but they are not necessarily so. Just as a book is entirely present in any of its copies, there is no a priori reason why a picture should not be fully represented in any of its reproductions. The distinction between non-mechanical and mechanical art has no meaning unless it means the distinction between good art and bad art.

The same is true of the distinction between fine art and industrial or applied art. It frequently rests upon class prejudice in favor of what is ornamental against what is useful. But the ornamental is useful or it would not have charm: that is, it would not please us if it did not serve us by ministering to our need. And the useful, that which is adapted to an end, always has charm to the really sophisticated as well as to the unsophisticated mind. This charm of utility, of adaptation, is the charm of art, which is nothing other than the fitting together of means and ends. It is art itself, whether one behold it in the galleries of the Louvre or see it in leaning over a parapet of the Seine watching the barges that ply up and down beneath the bridges, or the automobiles which stream back and forth across them.

Santayana says in his soliloquy on Dickens: "It is worth noting how such instrumentalities, which absorb modern life, are admired and enjoyed by Dickens, as they were by Homer. The poets ought not to be afraid of them; they exercise the mind congenially, and can be played with joyfully. Consider the black ships and the chariots of Homer, the coaches and river-boats of Dickens, and the aeroplanes of today; to what would an unspoiled mind turn with more interest?"[16] Nor are the poets afraid of them. Edna St. Vincent Millay has expressed the fascination of trains:

> The railroad track is miles away,
>   And the day is loud with voices speaking,
> Yet there isn't a train goes by all day
>   But I hear its whistle shrieking.
>
> All night there isn't a train goes by,
>   Though the night is still for sleep and dreaming,
> But I see its cinders on the sky,
>   And hear its engine steaming.
>
> My heart is warm with the friends I make,
>   And better friends I'll not be knowing,
> Yet there isn't a train I wouldn't take,
>   No matter where it's going.

A railroad train may seem as wonderful as a cathedral. Will one admit that the latter is art and not the former? What is art? Is not the one a "fitting together" as much as the other? Objectively, then, there seems no ground for discrimination. Subjectively? The emotional thrill when the ground trembles before an oncoming section of the Twentieth Century, when the headlight flashes around a curve, and the locomotive rushes by with a

[16] *Soliloquies in England,* p. 59.

roar, losing itself in the night, with its tremendous train like a roll of thunder in the wake of lightning—this thrill is produced by nothing in the thirteenth century! It cannot be objected that railroads are built for non-aesthetic ends, for the same is true of cathedrals and all great works of art. Art is an adaptation of instrumentalities which in themselves are non-aesthetic to ends which also are non-aesthetic. It *is* the adaptation, the arrangement, the fitting together itself which is aesthetic. Art and beauty exist only as a part of life: it is impossible to conceive of them apart from it. Aesthetic experience is always involved in a problematic situation of some sort, whether it arise adventitiously or by the agency of art.

It is in this fact that the distinction between fine art and other art can be justified, if at all. That is to say that since art always answers to some problem, it may be said that the finest art is that which corresponds to our deepest needs, representing the most vital values. Thus an ice wagon, however well done, which meets the minor need of hauling ice, is not as ravishing as a symphony which answers to the aspiration of the soul! Similarly, a train which solves the problem of traveling over the earth, though it is thrilling, is not as impressive as a cathedral which lifts one clear out of this world to another. Yet it is ultimately impossible to make distinctions in art on account of its mystical character which may at any time swallow them up. In any real work of art there is represented a complete synthesis of means and ends, of problem and answer, and to him who is sensitive to it all life is there, with love and death. The mystic sees God in the least of his works, and could see nothing more in the greatest. Whitman said the miracle of a mouse would stagger a host of infidels, and if the structure of an ice wagon were seen through a microscope or through the insight of a mystic the Cathedral of Chartres would not be more wonderful!

Beauty is everywhere and with equal magic for the eye which can see it. But the eye can see it only when it falls within the focus of a problematic situation. Such a situation may arise naturally by chance, or it may be induced by art. But outside of problems nothing detaches itself from the background to appeal to us; we move habitually through an undifferentiated continuum like somnambulists, unaware of the beauty all about us. Most things never attract our attention; they are like plain girls who are not noticed. But any girl will be noticed if she appear within a situation which centers attention upon her, or if such a situation be created for her by art. The plainest girl may become an object of aesthetic interest in the right gown, in the right hat, without her glasses. In the right setting she is like a figure in a painting which absorbs the beauty of the whole composition. This does not mean that she is then made to appear other than she is, for rather she is only then made to appear as she is, since it is only in the light of the aesthetic experience that anything ever really appears to us at all. The eye of the artist or the lover is not deceived in seeing beauty where others have missed it, for beauty is everywhere to the eye that can see it, and the glorious function of the artist is to persuade us of this fact. We can all see beauty in the belle of the ball, but he can make us see it even in the old courtesan.

Art directs our attention to values. Values are aesthetic so long as they are contemplated for their own sake—what the aestheticians mean by "disinterestedness," though it is really the state of profoundest interest. Values are attended to "for their own sake," they are appealing, they are beautiful, because they are the very factors to which some puzzle has sensitized us, the elements in a problematic situation which will release our response thereto. Aesthetic values are ultimate because they must be taken account of in the final solution—though they will then cease to be aesthetic, since the moment a solution is actually realized the attention is released and the values achieved are simply accepted without receiving any further regard. Thus the men a fraternity rushes are the values answering to the problem of perpetuating the chapter. They assume the dignity of aesthetic objects in drawing attention to themselves while they are being looked over and found to meet the requirements; but when they are safely pledged the attitude maintained toward them during the rushing season quickly subsides. When the problem is at least temporarily solved and experience redintegrated those aspects which had been conspicuous through their problematic character become taken for granted among our comfortable, established habits; they get broken in like old shoes which no longer shine as they did—yet neither do they hurt us nor make us fearful of hurting them. Much as we enjoy the aesthetic phase of experience we are pleasantly relieved after it is over, just as the sweetest sleep follows the sweetest excitements.

The moral attitude is concerned with concluding the solution of a problem; the scientific attitude deals with the means for its attainment; the attitude of day-dream or make-believe presents the values as if they had been attained; but the aesthetic experience stops with contemplation of the values for their own sake, without going on to actualize them, and without dreaming that they have already been achieved. To strive to realize them is to leave the aesthetic phase of experience for the moral or the scientific stage; to succeed in realizing them is to win surcease and sink back upon the couch of unconsciousness, whence all experience arose.

Yet this is only half true, for while the aesthetic experience may be located at a certain point within a problematic situation, actually that point includes the whole situation. The first uneasiness aroused by the difficulty, the first undirected and diffuse, impulsive responses to it, the later envisagement of the end and solution with the consequent intelligent concentration and direction of effort toward its attainment, with the concomitant sense of ease and facilitation—all of this goes into the aesthetic experience, is taken up into it, *aufgehoben,* as Hegel says, fused and harmonized in a balance and symmetry, a synthesis of stimulation and repose which is beauty. The aesthetic experience omits nothing; it is a mystical inclusiveness of everything in life. The moral and the scientific attitudes, along with day-dreaming, are merged within it. Taken alone, these other attitudes or phases within a problematic situation are not aesthetic, but taken all together they are nothing else. When art or life, or a unit of art or life is analyzed into its elements its beauty is dissolved. Beauty is completeness, wholeness, harmony. Aspiration is only half of it; consummation is only half of it. Neither is aesthetic by itself. The aesthetic moment is the midpoint in a problematic situation where they are both present at once. When that point is passed the spell is broken, consummation swallows up aspiration, the beauty of their perfect harmony is dissipated, the magic moment is gone.

If a young man be confronted with a girl who possesses values answering to his love problem his response is aesthetic so long as he is absorbed in admiring her; it ceases to be so if he make an acquisitive advance toward her. Hence the values she represents to him would be more safely aesthetic if embodied in marble or spread upon canvas, where it would be impossible to go beyond the point of contemplation, where aspiration and consummation are balanced. Or if she herself were hopelessly beyond reach she would remain aesthetic. "A perfect love is nourished by despair."[17] Aesthetic values are valuable because they reply to a problem, but they prefer to respond, like Echo, from afar. Their beauty fades or is forgotten if we profane them by destroying their distance and pull them from their pedestal. If we do so, like Pygmalion we may gain a wife but we lose our statue, though this may be the issue we desire. From the aesthetic point of view, however, values are not prized for their relation to problems, but problems them-

[17] Santayana.

selves are welcomed for their attendant values. In the moment of appreciation we would not consent to solving the problem that generates our vision, for then it too would be withdrawn. Yet this need not disturb us, since novel problems appear ahead for every problem solved, bringing new beauties, as every latitude left astern connotes new constellations in the sky. Thus a true marriage which continues to be a courtship sustains the beauty of love instead of destroying it, for it continues to be "an indissoluble bipolar tension," as Keyserling calls it, and that is a very problematic situation which it is difficult to maintain. But, as Spinoza says, all things excellent are as difficult as they are rare. What makes marriage difficult is the tendency to regard it as a consummation, and thus abolish its problematic character with its attendant aesthetic quality, which quickly brings satiety and boredom. The love problem remains, of course, but its value or beauty is then sought outside or else bitterly relinquished. Dewey says: "The infinite flippancy of the natural man is a standing theme for discourse by shrewd observers of human nature. Cultivated taste alone is capable of prolonged appreciation of the same object; and it is capable of it because it has been trained to a discriminating procedure which constantly uncovers in the object new meanings to be perceived and enjoyed."[18]

That is to say that values, to remain aesthetic, must arise within a situation which remains problematic. If we prize certain values it behooves us to cultivate the situation in which they grow, and not allow it to become barren. But there are situations which naturally

[18] *Experience and Nature,* p. 399.

continue to be fertile in values. Such is that of physical conduct in general, which, being constantly in adjustment, always retains a problematic character. It sensitizes us to stimuli which call out responses tending to maintain and refresh our organism. These stimuli are our physical values, and their attractiveness is as permanent as our physical problem. Automatically found in nature and in athletes, in art they are focused and objectified to facilitate our response. It is largely because we are ever seeking physical adjustment and balance that we find beautiful a landscape, a statue, a temple, or a symphony which gives us a harmony of physical values that enhances our visceral and circulatory response of respiration, equilibrium, and cardiac action.

To remain aesthetic our values must be somewhat removed from us so that we may contemplate them for their own sake, dispassionately, albeit with profound interest. Hence sight and hearing are the senses which usually present aesthetic values, for they are the distance senses, they reveal things somewhat detached and remote. "Taste and touch are too intimate, too immediately vital."[19] To see something as a thing of beauty we must for the time being become absolutely absorbed in regarding it, without embracing it or biting into it. This attitude is easiest to maintain toward something at a distance from us, and such a thing is likely to be constituted for the most part by sight or sound. It is more uncertain, more illusory, more problematic, than something within our grasp. Since we are not close enough to touch it or taste it, we are forced to study it,

[19] Jane Harrison, *Ancient Art and Ritual,* p. 131.

to contemplate it. What we firmly possess and have hold of forms part of our immediate, habitual, unimaginative experience. We are purblind to it. There is no mystery, no enchantment about it. Values always float beyond our reach; and from the aesthetic point of view a bird in the bush is worth two in the hand. It is because vision and audition furnish mediate rather than immediate experience that they provide most of our aesthetic experience. These perceptions operate at such long range that their objects must perforce be contemplated, in contrast to the objects within reach of the other senses, which are rarely contemplated, inasmuch as we simply have them, hold them, and tend to forget them. Our possessions do not challenge our attention; they do not arouse adoration and longing; the Grail itself did not become an object of quest until it seemed unattainable. That to which we aspire must ever be beyond us. Long ago Sappho said:

> I do not think with my two arms to touch the sky,
> I do not dream to do almighty things;
> So small a singing bird may never soar so high,
> To beat the sapphire fire with baffled wings.
>
> I do not think with my two arms to touch the sky,
> I do not dream by any chance to share
> With deathless Gods the bliss of Paphos they deny
> To men behind the azure veil of air.

And Santayana says today:

> I never asked of Heaven thou shouldst love me;
> As well ask Heaven's self that spreads above me
> With all his stars about my head to bend.
> It is enough my spirit may ascend
> And clasp the good whence nothing can remove me.

III

SENSUOUS ART AND LITERARY ART

We admire nature, athletes, and sensuous art because they provide the physical values corresponding to our physical problem. But our social, like our physical, conduct is also constantly in adjustment; hence we are always on the lookout for social as well as physical values. We look for them in social intercourse itself, in the human interest stories of the newspaper, in the motion pictures, in poetry and drama, but chiefly in the novel. That these agencies all supply hints for the understanding of social life and the conduct of it accounts for their popularity: but only the long, flexible form of the novel is adequate to the representation of the values of personality, the slow building up of character, which is the central part of our social problem. Most of our aesthetic values arise within the frames of these two general problems, the physical and the social, though any values become aesthetic when they are attended to solely for their own sake, without any ulterior purpose. Thus aesthetic experience is not a separate kind of experience. It occurs in any department of life at the moment when values, the cues for response to a situation, monopolize attention. It is the joyous moment when out of the perplexity of the problem we find just what we were (perhaps unconsciously) looking for. Art helps us to find values by representing them so that we can see them clearly. Physical values are the sphere of sensuous art, social values, of literary art. There is an aspect of the literary in sensuous art; and there is a phase of the sensuous in literature. Literary art is increasing in importance with the rising importance of social conduct in civilization. The novel has become the dominant literary form because it most adequately represents social values. The joy of sensuous art lies in the response of the physical self; the zest of the novel lies in the response of the social self. The novel is then to be judged by its satisfaction to our social capacities. Sensuous art stimulates primarily the body; it is athletic; the novel stimulates primarily the personality, it is social.

This distinction is based upon the functional dualism that is called psycho-physical, and not upon the metaphysical dualism of Descartes (see Table I). To make plain that the latter is not in question it will suffice to sketch how that false doctrine was developed and how it was dissolved. It was due to science and Descartes. Descartes was so impressed with the certainty of mathematical science that he made its method the criterion of philosophical truth. He measured the world with its rule. In so doing he left out what was not extended. Thus he literally had no place to put Thought. Yet she of course had given him the whole idea, and he was not ungrateful, but he was embarrassed. To calm his conscience he gave her a sort of pension, and did not shut her out entirely. Then he hurried back to play with his new toy, the physical world. Democritus, Leonardo, and Copernicus had been fascinated with something of the sort, and after Galileo, Kepler, and Newton

TABLE I

THE METAPHYSICAL DUALISM OF RENÉ DESCARTES

Thought	Extension
Mind	Matter
Secondary qualities: taste, touch, color, sound, etc.	Primary qualities: extension, figure, motion
Religion, art and all values	Mechanism, materialism, business
	Descartes developed this side so much more than the other that it crowded the other out of the world, especially after the triumphs of mathematical science in the work of Copernicus, Kepler, Galileo, and Newton. People began to think that reality is on this side,
that this side is ideal, sentimental, not worthy serious attention, left to women and effeminate men. But everything which men most prize, including all their values and their thoughts, belong here. Therefore if this is not real, man himself is not real, and has no place in the world. But man is in the world, and just as real as anything in it.	
	Therefore this mechanistic materialistic view is inadequate. The advance of science shows that it has truth in it, but it is only half the story.

[*Table continued on page 56*]

TABLE I—*Continued*

The modern view is that this old division is unreal, that there is no such separation into two worlds which cannot be reconciled. Cf. Whitehead, *Science and the Modern World,* that the concept of organism is superseding that of mechanism in science, and this concept allows for all the vital factors which mechanism leaves out, and is therefore truer. For the world is just what it is no matter if mechanism denies half of it—*tant pis* for mechanism.

had perfected it, thinkers could hardly think of anything else. In the beginning it had to be wound up now and then or even pushed along, and sometimes it would break down. They often had to ask God to help them with it, which he always did. But at length they got it so it would go by itself. Now they could all jump in and ride, with nothing to do but observe and admire it and hold on to their hats. They hardly looked where they were going. They never thought to think of God when they did not need him any more (and there was no room for Thought), until someone noticed that he had dropped out. Poetry fainted. Last thing they knew their souls blew away; then they lost their minds; and finally they all fell out. They landed in a fairy place made of all the things they had thrown away as unessential to their machine, including themselves, their minds, their souls, their God, their thought, their religion, art and poetry. Still dazed from their ride and their fall, some of them insisted that while this was all very lovely, it was purely ideal and imaginary, that nothing was real except that man-made machine which had run away with them; some said they did not care if this was a dream, since it was much more satisfying than that other experience which they had escaped; while some went so far as to say that this ideal world was alone real and that it was high time they waked up from that whirling nightmare of mechanism.

This is almost exactly what happened. Descartes is to blame for it, because while he neither invented nor perfected the infernal machine of Mechanism, he patented it, so to speak; he made patent to everyone its wonderful qualities, saying nothing of the danger and absurdity in it, which it is fair to say he himself did not suspect. After Descartes people had either to get in it or stay out of it; they could not ignore it. Finally the thing ran wild with those who were still in it and unseated them all. The objects most obviously unessential to its mechanism were the first to go. They were called secondary qualities, in contrast to the qualities primary to it, which were reduced to extension, figure, and motion. Men themselves were thus found to be mere bundles of secondary qualities, and so they inevitably had to go by the board into limbo. There was no place for human beings in the non-human mechanical world asserted to be the real world.

This was not satisfactory, for while limbo might be a delightful place at first, it was felt to be unreal and therefore ultimately uninteresting. The more daring decided to try their mechanism again, but this time to remodel it, upholster it with those qualities which had formerly seemed unessential to it, but which they now realized they could not exist without, and so make their machine fit for human occupancy. After all, men had made it as it was, and they could remake it. They could now see that the mechanical principle was true, but that it was not the whole truth: the other things men lived by were equally true and much more important to their happiness. They concluded then to use mechanism for what it was worth and keep it in its place; they swore not to let it run away with them again, and vowed they would never again throw away their most precious possessions, themselves included, for the sake of mechanical consistency. The "physical world" of mathematical science was now recognized to have been an abstraction, and hence the Cartesian dualism between it and the things of thought was seen to be artificial and unreal. Science was not discredited, for it was largely due to the refining of science itself that the earlier scientific view of the world was shown to be inadequate; it was its own crudity which had necessitated discarding the fine things of life, and now it was its own new refinement which really reinstated them more securely than before. The new theories of evolution and relativity showed values to be inherent in nature rather than subjective and precarious. Poetic insight was vindicated by science; the poet and the scientist were reconciled by the same philosophy of creative evolution.

To say, then, that nature and art are refreshing to man's physical self, that they present physical values to him, is not to use "physical" in the abstract and recent sense of mathematical science (which has been cut under by more recent biological science), but to use it in the ancient and athletic sense of the animal organism. The physical self is here thought of as the body contrasted with the social or civilized self: it is not thought of as a machine of mass particles over against a pure spirit, neither of these notions being tenable to contemporary thought. What is meant by saying that art is physical or sensuous, while literature is social, is that we get from the former more of the stimulus which nature and athletes give us, while we get from the latter more of the stimulus which society gives us, though neither stimulus is ever pure and unadulterated by the other. Art and literature do not take sides in the obsolete Cartesian dualism, but in the ever present psycho-physical dualism, that between the physical self and what is regarded as the higher, more spiritual self, the self that lives in society, which is constituted by its contacts with other personalities, the self that does not live by bread alone, which arises in a body, but escapes by its power of imagination to other bodies, or transcends them all to contemplate God, freedom, and immortality. In terms of this psycho-physical dualism art is on the side of the athletes and literature on the side of the angels.

Sensuous art represents the values answering to the problems of the physical self. Its plastic form is an integration of all the plastic qualities of color, light, line, and space, facilitating a corresponding integration in the responses of the body to these stimuli. But literature presents the values in the problems of the social self, problems of love, religion, education, politics, and law. Sensuous art also ministers widely to the social self, but it cannot compete in this sphere with the social art of literature. If it could, people would not read novels as they do, hardly knowing pictures except as illustrations of stories. When the social self was less developed and complex, art was able to satisfy its needs; but with the modern intensification of self-consciousness the social self has come to require literature. And it is interesting that lovers of non-literary art, recognizing its inability to rival literature on this terrain, have given up the contest almost altogether, declaring that literary or social values are foreign to sensuous art, which is properly concerned solely with physical or plastic values. They say that only the title of a work of plastic art is literary, its subject is always sensuous. Plastic art, they say, affects the social self indirectly through its effect upon the senses: it can thus induce a mood or state of mind, but it is not its province to attempt more than that in the social sphere. Enlightened art critics seem concerned almost entirely with overcoming naïve interest in the superficial literary aspect of a work of art, directing attention to its proper plastic qualities. Modern artists are constantly learning new things about plastic form: their work is simplified when they are relieved of responsibility for literary values; and appreciation by the public is facilitated when it is educated to concentrate upon the heart of the matter, no longer confused and befuddled by a mistaken preoccupation with values which are secondary or even irrelevant to plastic form.

There is here no intent, then, to divorce sensuous from social values. They are as close as body and mind: just as an effect upon the one always affects the other, so physical values always have social value, and vice versa. If a painting refreshes the body it thereby refreshes the mind; and if a novel stimulates the mind it cannot fail to tone up the body. All that is here intended is to establish a distinction of emphasis. Plastic art is primarily sensuous; literature, primarily social. In the larger sense of the word, literature is as much an art as any, since it also is a representation of a problematic situation in the aesthetic phase; but the problems which it deals with are social rather than physical.

Literature is largely a linkage of lines, a sequence of sounds; but it is essentially a harmony of thoughts. The sensuous form of art still has importance in literature, for in becoming intellectual and social beings we do not cease to be physical. When we think, we do so in terms of our old unthinking life, and our ancient organic adjustments of respiration and equilibrium are not suspended when we rise to spiritual aspiration and a larger social balance. Thus an appeal to our social personality makes a strategic approach by first satisfying our basic physical self; that is why literature is ever solicitous of sensuous form. To be successful a writer must be seductive, because it is by propitiating the sentinels of the senses, by bewitching the bodyguard, that he may gain access to the person he finally wishes to influence. It is impossible to reach the mind directly, without entering through the body. Because our minds are embodied, messages to them must assume forms which can pass the gates of the body, or they move us not.

Simple cries and plaints are the beginning of literature, and they have a direct physical effect. When a man pleads with another or endeavors to persuade him he employs intonations and cadences which play upon his fibers to elicit an instinctive response. When a savage wishes to tell his children the great deeds of the past, or answer their questions about creation, he uses his most expressive sounds, gesticulations, and rhythms, perhaps chanting and striking a musical instrument; and he makes poetry. When poetry is read aloud it is evident that the prevailing meter, iambic pentameter, is that of common speech, and that other meters have special effects, solemn, joyful, or sad, which are unconsciously used in ordinary conversation. Experiments in the physiology of poetry have shown that whereas adults breathe easily once in ten syllables, this span is too long for children: hence children's rhymes are written in shorter lines which are jerky to their elders.

But literature would be merely a limited kind of music, as indeed it tends to be with some poets, were it only a matter of sensuous form. In so far as a writer is a musician he is tempted to become exclusively interested in the sound of his words. This is dangerous, because in order to use words he must be interested in something else; he must have something to write about. If he becomes more absorbed in words than in the things and thoughts they represent, his words lose meaning and in so far cease to be words; they become mere sounds. Then he had better put down his pen and take up a fiddle. A composer or plastic artist may forget literary values in his occupation with sensuous form; he really has only one horse to guide. But a writer has two horses to his chariot, Physis and Psyche, which must run together as synchronously as body and soul.

With the growth of civilization and the concomitant expansion of the social self, man looks more than ever to literature for inspiration, and when it fobs him off with that which "fine art" can better give, it fails him. That it has been his help in past ages is evidenced by the discoveries of the great folklore of the world. For a while "fine art" seemed dominant because word of mouth was then too slight a vehicle to transport thought through time, compared to monuments of stone, carvings in rock, and colors on canvas, despite the fact that the latter represent social values only as ancillary to the physical. But since 1450 the world has known that nothing outlives words on paper, or spreads like them to all the countries of the compass.

Words being the easiest medium of thought, now that they can readily be printed, disseminated, and read, it is no wonder that literature is in the ascendant. It is true, as Leonardo says, that a picture speaks directly to men of all languages without an interpreter, but it speaks chiefly to the physical self through its plastic form. What message it may have for the social self must be an old story, or a simple one, familiar and conventionalized, as in religious art, or an interpreter is needed. Carpaccio's wonderful sequence of pictures illustrating the legend of St. Ursula tells a story all the way around the room, but only to him who knows her life or follows the story in his guidebook. If there is much social, that is literary, meaning in a work of painting, sculpture, music, or any non-literary art, words are needed to express it; a program or explanation must be appended. These arts can suggest and recall much of social import; they can *show* a great deal through signs and symbols and through inducing moods; but they cannot talk to any man in his mother-tongue. If we pause before a work of art, wondering what it means apart from its plastic effect, the aid of literary art must be called in to give a satisfactory answer. So it was that the great, dark allegories of Tintoret became absorbing to Ruskin when his literary genius had figured out their meaning, or a meaning for them, and fascinating to the public after it had read the interpretations of Ruskin. Though this kind of literary interpretation is discouraged today by art critics, it is legitimate when one considers that, in a day when people did not read, art was expected to give them religious instruction. The mosaics in St. Mark's were intended to tell the illiterate the stories of the Old and New Testaments. Now, however, when the people have direct access to literature, it is natural that they should turn to it for literary values, and it is accordingly proper that literary criticism of art should be diminished, though it has historical importance in the case of works of art whose original purpose was certainly as much literary as it was plastic. But literary values cannot now be the center of interest in a painting when there is a bookstore or a library in every community; a work of non-literary art must now stand or fall on its non-literary artistic merit.

A social or literary element is not denied in any art but the purely decorative, nor is the sensuous texture denied in literature. Sometimes painting almost becomes narrative, as in Carpaccio's "Life of St. Ursula"; sometimes narrative nearly becomes painting, as in Flaubert's *Madame Bovary*. Art has a wider power to the extent that it can stimulate the social as well as the physical self. Indeed, we almost always look for some social import in a work of art even when we know that its artistry lies essentially in the sensuous sphere, and in its great periods art has always subserved some social purpose. The weakness of much modern art lies in its lack of purpose beyond giving a sensuous impression, which by itself cannot possibly absorb a social being. Vernon Lee says: "No one except an art critic sees a new picture or statue without first asking 'What does it represent?' shape-perception and aesthetic empathy arising incidentally in the examination which this question leads to. The truth is that even the art critic is oftenest brought into enforced contemplation of the artistic shape by some other question which arises from his particular bias: 'By whom? of what precise date?' "[1]

The approach to literature is the opposite: we are first attracted by its charm, and only then attend to what it says and means. The spell of sensuous art steals over us while we are asking what it represents; the message of literature is whispered while the senses are lulled by its voice. The best logic only half convinces without attractive form; while nonsense will more than half persuade if the sound of it captivate the heart. Logic carries a case only after argument, whereas pleasing expression is immediately infectious and wins almost without reason, because it charms before the words are out of its mouth. Scientific writing often sacrifices grace in the effort to run most directly to the intellectual goal, but a great scientist is often an artist as well, whose thought is suffused with feeling which is not lost in being explicit and precise, though he is exceptional if he can write like Leonardo or Fabre. Literature as such is dedicated to

[1] *The Beautiful*, p. 137.

the expression of the whole of human life in so far as that is possible, and since the intellect is a superstructure to the deep emotions, it is to the ministry of the latter that the art of literature is first called. Literature must satisfy sense before sensibility; it must caress the ear before it may salute the soul. The vividness of life cannot be expressed in thin intellectual concepts, which are only its shells and husks.

It is sometimes said that philosophy should confine its expression to the supposedly dry style of pure science, imputing it a fault in a philosopher to write exceedingly well lest he dazzle the understanding and distract it from the argument. This contention might be correct if philosophy were simply a logical escalator which anyone could climb in a hurry; or a *scala santa* which the faithful could climb on their knees; but it is more like a ladder let down from heaven in a dream; it begins in wonder and it ends in vision. And to express itself it needs every rung in the ladder of language. To those who understand it, philosophy is the highest literature; it awakens in them the deepest response of their being, because it most adequately represents the values of their profoundest problems. Instead of being abstract and empty, as Hegel would say, in it all the concreteness of life is taken up.

The problems of most people, however, are sufficiently dealt with in the novel, and that is why it is popular. Child's rhymes and stories are enjoyed only in childhood or during those moods in which we lapse into a childish attitude. On the other hand most people rarely rise to the level of the most mature poetry and philosophy, though all have moments in which they can live above their usual plane and enjoy what would bore their ordinary selves. In general, though people dream of roaming, they do not wander far from home. Unfamiliar emotions, profound or foreign thoughts, are rarely visited. Even a story must not only be translated into the local language; it must be given local color before it can really be brought home to the people, unless it be an utterly simple tale with nothing to stamp it as outlandish, like the story of Joseph. Extraordinary books are not widely read unless circumstances have made them ordinary, like the Bible, and even then they are more widely spread than read. Those books which are really popular are those which minister to present and pressing needs of the body and soul. As the problems of most people are the same, so are the values which they seek, so are the books in which they find them.

Literature is chiefly concerned with social values. This explains why such scant attention is given it in most books on aesthetics: it is out of bounds for a criticism of mere sensuous form, to which works on aesthetics are too often limited. If the test of sensuous art is in its effect upon the physical self, the test of literature must be in its effect upon the social self. Those plastic forms are beautiful which arouse a harmonious physical response; those are ugly which, while they stimulate a response, are so deformed that the response is frustrated and baffled. So those books are beautiful which bring out a deep social response of sympathy and tenderness, a new level of love and understanding, a new equilibrium of the personality upon a broader base. Those books are ugly which stimulate narrow interests out of proportion to the wider, which do not summon the whole personality into new activity upon a higher plane, but tend to lower it and weaken it by a meretricious appeal to particular impulses. Experience is required to tell the difference, but he who has felt the release and exhilaration to be had in good books will feel cramped and inhibited in those which appeal to only part of his self, or fail to stimulate his highest possibilities and raise him to the apex of his being.

A statue as lumpish as the figures slumping all about us, a picture as ill composed as the scenes which ordinarily bore us, is no more invigorating than they, and we are rightly irritated by it, for the *raison d'être* of art is the enhancement of life. Similarly, a novel as dull and unmeaning as much of life appears to be is futile. But a statue that catches our breath and takes us up on tiptoe, like the Apollo Belvedere, or a novel which lifts us out of our littleness to a universal sympathy, like *Anna Karenina*—that is worth while.

The peculiar value of literature is that with its discursiveness it yet retains immediate artistic charm. Thought is infused into the form, and the form is suffused through the thought. "When we talk of books conceived well and written badly, we cannot mean anything other than that in these books there are parts, pages, periods, and propositions, well thought and well written, and others, perhaps less important, badly thought and badly written, not really thought and therefore not really written. . . . . How could a proposition be thought clearly and written obscurely?"[2] When a writer learns to dive backward into a sentence, turn on himself like a swimmer and slide out the other way, he is mastering thought as well as expression. The two are indissoluble.

We are more aware of this in literature than in "fine art," because few of us have creative experience in painting, or sculpture, or music, whereas all of us express ourselves in words from the moment we find our tongues: we know the difficulties involved, and spontaneously applaud when we see them overcome. We are at home here; we have practice and knowledge; we are not helpless hypocrites, as we so often are at a concert or a gallery, where we hardly know good from bad unless told by someone who may not know either. A man who reads nothing but the newspaper knows more about literature than most people know about painting and sculpture; it is not too hard for him to step up to magazines and books. But is the man who enjoys the comic strips prepared to appreciate art? The answer is easy if art be restricted to the contents of museums; but this is not fair, since in the wider sense all fitting together, all work of skill, is art, and any of it may be "fine." Thus a man with no taste in pictures may have a nice appreciation of athletics or automobiles or electrical devices or business organization or statesmanship, etc. There is no field of human interest closed to art and aesthetic appreciation, nor any in which they are monopolized. If the "fine arts," so called, are finer than other manifestations of art, it cannot be simply that they ex-

[2] Croce, *Estetica,* p. 28.

hibit finer skill, but that they represent higher values, or a higher synthesis of values. Sometimes they justify their fine title by doing so, but not always. Perhaps statesmanship is the highest art, and real statesmen the men, as Santayana suggests, who should be hailed as the greatest artists or poets.

But present circumstances are such that literary men, especially novelists, get the most *kudos*. Their works appear to give the synthesis of values most helpful in contemporary life. The novel ministers better to the modern self than any other art, because it includes every other. It can take us into the very presence of nature and the sea; it offers pictures as effective as any ever painted; it leads us into temples equaling those achieved by architecture; it suggests harmonies unheard, which is the best that music can do; it takes up into itself all other literary forms; and besides stealing the thunder of the so-called "fine arts," it borrows from all the arts of life, representing the values of all human activities and interests, love, religion, education, recreation, politics, economics, law, science, and philosophy; finally, the novel is supreme in representing the sovereign art of life itself, to which all other arts are contributory.

IV

WHY WE READ NOVELS

A philosophic basis for criticism is necessary to separate the good novel from the bad, but in aesthetics, as in ethics, there is no absolute standard. Of two ways of life, of two kinds of novel, those who have tried both may judge, and they must be tolerant of differing temperaments, knowing that the end for each person is self-realization in social harmony. A novel is a way of life, and the best way is that leading to the fullest life. In the novel, as in the world, things are neither good nor bad in themselves, but are relative to minds. Though none wishes to be miserable, no lover of Victor Hugo should object to living with him among *Les Misérables;* though none wishes to be bored, no admirer of Marcel Proust should demur to living with him among the bored upper classes. One should be willing to spend a whole life in misery or luxury to see what these authors see, for life has no tang or taste except through the forms of an understanding mind. Each makes his own world in a measure, seeing things with his own eyes; but it is illuminating to share the vision of those who are keener sighted. Like climbing a tree or a hill, it is not only pleasant in itself, but may help us on our way. A good novel not only affords a good time, but it objectifies values, and that is the real secret of its attraction. The novelist does not solve our problems and he should not try, for the aesthetic experience consists in pure contemplation of values and disappears when a solution is attempted. A novelist who makes the attempt sacrifices his art to propaganda.

As our problems differ with age, sex, and occupation, so will our taste in novels vary; but in so far as our main problems remain the same we should be able to agree upon the great novels which objectify our universal values. If the novel, or any art, concerns itself with values which are evanescent or insignificant, it cannot be permanent or universal. But great art fits fundamental needs, and that is why the response to it is direct and unhesitating. Those books which in the past have answered to elemental needs have come to be honored as classics. But in so far as problems do change, each generation must edit the list of classics for itself. We must not follow the old list blindly; we must add to it and cancel from it. If we scorn the classics we throw away our culture, for new classics seldom spring up in a night. The new books which do appear often satisfy only particular needs, ignoring the ancient and profound conditions of our being. Some new novels are good, but there would not be so many bad ones if their scope were more often compared with that of the classics in their day. Those who have known the satisfaction in books of fundamental value are safe from inferior works, but those whose taste is constantly vitiated by the week's best seller have difficulty in appreciating the deeper charm of the best sellers of the ages. How much the classics have been defamed by awkward teaching, and how many have come back to them with delight after years of truancy, we do not know; but many who have returned to them have testified to the joy they have found.

In admitting, however, that the list of the classics is only an approximate guide to reading we confess the need of a more rational criterion. We should be able to know a good book when we read it, regardless of its reputation, and be able to tell how we know it. A basis for criticism of sensuous art is found in its physical effects; for literature it will be found in social effects. The social self, seldom adequately stimulated either in intercourse with others or in communion with itself, has a chance in the best novels to live to the height of its capacity, and that is the criterion of their quality.

Men read even the worst of novels because they supply something lacking in their lives, because they satisfy a hunger. Menéndez y Pelayo comes to this conclusion in reflecting upon the vogue of the romance of knight-errantry in the sixteenth century. He says that Juan de Valdés, "one of the finest and most delicate spirits, and one of the most admirable prose writers of Spanish literature, Valdés, Hellenist and Latinist, friend and correspondent of Erasmus, catechist of august ladies, teacher of Julia Gonzaga and Victoria Colonna, after saying in his *Diálogo de la lengua* that the books of knight-errantry, excepting the *Amadis* and some others, 'besides being very untruthful, are so very badly written . . . . that there is no stomach strong enough to read them,' confesses immediately afterward that he has read them *all*. 'Ten years, the best of my life, which I wasted in palaces and courts, I did not employ myself in any exercise more virtuous than reading these lies, in which I took such delight that I ate with my hands among them.' "[1] Menéndez y Pelayo goes on to say that:

> The explanation of this phenomenon appears very simple. The novel fulfils one of its ends when it excites and satisfies the instinct of curiosity, even though it be puerile; when it squanders the resources of invention, though they be bad and vulgar; when it entertains us with a flood of adventures and prodigious events, even though badly put together. Every man has hours when he is a child, and he is unfortunate who does not have them. The perspective of an ideal world is always alluring, and the force of its prestige is such that one can hardly conceive of the human race without some kind of novels or stories, oral or written. Failing good ones, they read the bad, and this was the case with the books of knight-errantry in the sixteenth century and the principal reason for their exit.

To understand further this craving for novels, good or bad, it will be well to consider the nature of human personality. It begins to develop in the play of the child when he takes over the rôles of those about him,[2] for that is what child's play is for the most part: playing parent, doctor, visitor, tradesman. The personality is composed of the rôles which have been acquired, and it has to be built up little by little. It is not an endowment, but an achievement. One can become a member of society only by learning the rôles of the other members: this is the function of the imaginative play of children. Games are play controlled by rules. In order to play baseball in any position it is necessary to imagine one's

[1] *Estudios de Crítica Literaria,* Cuarta Serie, pp. 47, 48.

[2] This line of thought is taken from the class lectures in social psychology by Professor George Herbert Mead.

self in all the other positions. The first baseman has to know what the pitcher and the batter and the fielder are doing in order to co-ordinate with them; he has to put himself in their place. Getting along with other people always consists in doing this, taking their rôles. In so far as one does this one cannot make a mistake, because by putting one's self in the other's place one responds to one's own stimuli as the other does, and thereby anticipates the response of the other, checking and changing one's own behavior to make it appropriate. One hears one's own voice exactly as one's hearers do, and modulates the tone of it accordingly. To see one's self as others see one is to be successful in society, and this is done by identifying one's self with others, by taking their rôles. The self is social. It is built up by taking in other selves, and they constitute it literally, for if they were taken away it would cease to be itself. Allowing for initial differences in the organism, differences in personality are due to different social contacts. The richest personality is the one with the widest experience, enabling its possessor to do the right thing in every company, because, possessing the rôles of other people, he knows what they will do and how to meet it. Such a person preserves everywhere the poise which those of limited social experience keep only at home. People are at ease at home with their familiars because they have taken each other's rôles and know each other's parts, but it is possible to extend indefinitely the circle in which one is at home, simply by increasing one's repertory of rôles. Then, besides liking to be at home, people like to get away from home, and this also is accomplished by taking over the rôles of others. Thus in his play the child not only impersonates parts which establish him in his own house and neighborhood; he also takes on those which enable him to escape: those of Indians, pirates, knights, and kings.

For adults day-dreaming takes the place of play, but it is essentially the same thing, a taking over of the rôles of others. And here again the function of this process is twofold: first to make one feel at ease in one's group, and second to enable one to transcend the group. Some day-dreaming is a rehearsal for coming situations in everyday life; but some of it is an escape. Novels are a still further elaboration of play: those are realistic which bring us closer to our workaday world; those are romantic which release us from it; those are great which do both.

People who are perfectly adjusted, who are at home in the world and feel no hunger for anything better or different, do not read novels. Why should they waste their time on idle tales? They are like the incurious Romans who had no novels, because they were entirely satisfied with themselves and with Rome. They might have wondered how the barbarians lived who were paraded through their streets, or how the rabble lived in their streets, and welcomed novels about them. But they were satisfied, and if they were bored there was the arena for that. Those who read novels are people who do not fit, who are discontent, restless, romantic, uncertain of the world and of themselves. They are all people who seek something better, who are dissatisfied with things as they are, who are kept young and curious and alert by their intelligence, their awareness of possibilities, who are looking for different ways of life and other ways of organizing their own lives. Novels help them to adjust themselves to their circumstances, and to escape from them.

Another way of putting it is that people seek reality, they want to know what the world is like, what is really worth while in it. When they lived in small, stable groups there was no question about this, because reality is social, and in a group where all are adjusted and agreed the question does not come up. But in our society there are many different groups living side by side and intermingling with their different views and beliefs, so that they are all prevented from being dogmatic and certain that they possess the whole truth. Each group is critical and skeptical of the other and consequently of itself, for it is impossible to believe in the presence of skeptics as one would without them, and some doubt is cast all the way around. The children are taught one thing at home, another thing at school, and another thing at Sunday school. In high school they get more mixed up, and in college they do not know what to think. As they move from one social milieu to another they find very different ideas and standards of taste. They discover that some people utterly discount what other people prize. This makes them think and wonder. It makes them look about, gathering suggestions and cues. It makes them read the papers, go to the movies, and take up novels, for these are the agencies most ready with helps and hints for dealing with the problematic situation in which they find themselves.

Galsworthy's *Forsyte Saga* is a good illustration. To the Forsytes property is the real thing and "style" is the sign of it. But young Bosinney, representing artists, is indifferent to this view of reality, wherefore the Forsytes regard him as irregular and dangerous, and droll George Forsyte dubs him the Buccaneer. Then there is Val Dartie who says that if horses are no good nothing is; but his precious Mayfly filly seems to lose reality when Prosper Profond is by, the uncomfortable foreign gentleman who finds nothing in anything. There is Jack Cardigan who believes in "keeping fit"; but Prosper Profond says, "What's the use of keepin' fit?"

Yet he and his cynical kind who seem to form a group without any values really have principles about which they are not skeptical, such as shrewdness, blandness, sophistication; and they are not half so hard on others as they are on themselves; they put on their smoothness and swagger to mask their emptiness; their jibes against the beliefs and virtues of others are born of envy; their gospel of disillusion is reminiscent of the fox who lost his tail and then tried to persuade his fellows to cut off theirs; they scoff at others lest they sneer at themselves. Vice cannot endure virtue, because it has an inferiority complex toward it. Hence it tries to pull it down to its own level. Yet as far as possible the wicked try to appear like the just: it is only by assuming the protective coloring of decency that they can survive. They cannot even get along with themselves except in so far as they pretend to be just with one another. Evil is negative and cannot exist at all except under the guise of good. The honor among thieves is desperate; it is the last ditch. They are self-conscious of their code in the face of the surrounding opposition of society, and this opposition eats into their own souls. Honest men are not so touchy about honor, because they are at one with their world. But the antisocial person not only has to face suspicion and distrust at large; he also lives in constant dread of betrayal from behind and from within. In lieu of simple trust he has to rely on terrible oaths which are really the less binding the more dreadful they appear. Those who have broken faith with honest folk feel no real obligation to keep faith with their own ilk, except as it be momentarily expedient. Only the social is solid and secure; the antisocial is divided against itself; it is negative; it tends to dissolve and disappear. While this is most obvious in the extreme case of the criminal, it is verifiable in the case of anyone. The self is social; it comes into existence through a group, and it can continue to live only in society; where it goes against the group it defeats itself, unless it is thereby asserting its solidarity with another group. A self can be no more stable than the group or groups to which it belongs; if it belongs to a gang which is utterly at odds with the larger organization of society, it is not secure; if it belongs to several cliques which negate each other, it cannot be well knit. It is only by participating in, and identifying itself with, the most social groups that the self can achieve its fullest realization. Truly social groups are those which supplement and support each other. The best society would be one composed of units various enough for stimulus and similar enough for harmony. Reality is social, and exists over against the antisocial or unreal. The real things to us are those which are made such by the support of the group to which we belong. Our language, our religion, is made real by our group. Everyone who speaks a language gives life to it; if no one speaks it it dies. Everyone who worships a god contributes to the light of his divinity; when his followers fall away the twilight settles about him.

Thought itself is social. A thinker trained in mathematics will seek truth through its procedure and will be prone to regard other methods as less reliable. Thus Royce said that Hegel missed the real nature of the self in being contemptuous of the mathematical statement of it, calling it barren *Calcul.* Hegel scorned mathematics, thinking it nothing but theory, while he believed his own dialectic to reveal the truth of being. Royce said: "But if *alle Theorie* is, after all, *grau,* and *grün des Lebens Goldener Baum,* the philosopher, as himself a thinker, merely shares with his colleague, the mathematician, the fate of having to deal with dead leaves and sections torn or cut from the tree of life, in his toilsome effort to make out what the life is. The mathematician's interests are not the philosopher's. But neither of the two has a monopoly of the abstractions; and in the end . . . . each of them can learn from the other."[3] Still, each feels his own ground to be more solid than that of the other. For Plato mathematical forms showed the nature of reality. For Aristotle they did not. The two had different approaches to reality, socially determined: Plato was trained as a mathematician, Aristotle as a physician.

[3] Royce, Supplementary Essay to Vol. I of *The World and the Individual,* p. 526.

In some groups reality is interpreted neither in terms of mathematics nor logic nor medicine. To a large degree each sex has its own reality, each age, each profession and calling. Each puts life into its own terms, its own slang. The sailor says of a fat man: "A heavy-beamed craft that!" The stockman says of the city doctor's office: "A good place to winter in!" Not only slang, but all technical vocabularies express the interest of a group. The "best English" is that of the "best people," or it is the dialect of the "best writers." To each group the idiom of the other seems strange and even perverse. It is hard to believe that foreigners can converse in their outlandish tongue as we do in ours.

When different groups come together their members are forced to see that reality is social; but it is impossible to participate equally in the reality of every group even when it is recognized. William James says a man cannot be a philosopher, a lady-killer, and *bon vivant* all at once. What a relief, he says, to give up pretensions to Greek or music and settle on one thing, like psychology. But whatever a man ignores, he must identify himself with something, and what gives reality to anything whatsoever is the group which believes in it. As Shaw says, the Middle Ages believed in holy water and we believe in vaccine. Some of us are devoted to baseball and some to bridge. Sportsmen who care for nothing else put faith in sport; they know all about it, talk it, spend time on it. They make a listener feel foolish if he has never heard of their champions and their records, although most people never did hear of them or would care if they had. A coterie cultivates special interests and is stimulated by outside indifference or ignorance, like a secret society, like any society at all. Its altar fires are precious to it because *it* keeps them burning.

Yet most people are not entirely absorbed in any group. They keep trying to fit in more closely and at the same time keep an eye out for a possible escape. The novel helps them do both, and that is why it is popular. But while it is a great aid to life, it is a poor substitute for it. Since it objectifies values that are real in life, to leave life to dwell in fiction is to lose the sense of values and consequently the taste for novels themselves. Novels for their own sake are as insipid as any art for its own sake. Art gets its value from its relationship to non-aesthetic experience. Art refers back to a problem which generated its values, and ahead to the solution which will degenerate them.

Values are the projections of problems. It is the weak who want strength, the poor who want wealth, the weary who want rest, the young who want to grow older, the old who want to grow younger. The art which appeals to a person represents the values he needs; it is almost an infallible index to his character. It is fallible, however, to the extent that character is not fixed and can change. Otherwise criticism would be vain. If people came to what they crave as naturally as cattle come to salt, if they avoided what is harmful as instinctively as a dog shies from tobacco, they would not need advice, and they do not, as much as some suspect. Give them the different ancestors, the different bodies and minds which they need, and they will not need admonition; leave them as they are and they will not heed it. Much criticism is like remonstrating with the deaf that it would be a wonderful thing for them if they would listen to music, or with the blind that it would be a blessing to them to look at pictures. On the other hand there are many who do not realize that they could see or hear with a little guidance, and these the critic can help. As necessary as the tutor to teach one how to read is the critic to teach one what to read. People do not just naturally learn to read, but they read naturally enough after they have learned; people do not naturally appreciate the better books and the other refinements of life before their taste has been formed, but they naturally prefer them after they have learned to. Taste for fine literature is no more artificial than, and just as natural as, taste for olives. There are, of course, people constitutionally incapable of assimilating some foods; so there are some inherently unable to appreciate some things in art and literature. But as most people learn to imbibe other liquids than milk and water, and even to partake of solid food, so they also learn to digest spiritual fare less simple than the pabulum of their infancy. The baby's first hunger is solely for milk; but as his feeding is modified his hunger becomes complicated until milk is not enough, until even olives are desired. So a man's thirst drives him to drink water; but if fire is put in his water, and he likes it, presently plain water will not satisfy him.

A new liking becomes just as natural as the old, and often more imperious. It may be harmful, when it is the part of wisdom to moderate or eliminate it. In cases of spiritual indigestion dieting is just as important as ever. In reading, as in eating, one man's meat is another man's poison, and it is more serious to abuse a weak mind than a weak stomach. Children, at least, should not drink moonshine, nor should the mentally immature indulge in its literary counterpart. When taste is diverted from its pristine state it may be converted to something better or perverted to something worse, and if men get to a point where they cannot live without that which they cannot live with, they may have to go clear back to milk and water to save themselves.

The light of truth has always its shadow; an increase in intelligence makes it possible to become either better or worse; one discards innocence for vice or for virtue; man ceases to be an animal to become a devil or an angel. The worst evil and the best good are of the mind, and both are most fully represented in literature. Hence he who learns to read takes his soul in his own hands to blacken or to whiten it, according as he turns the pages of Pietro Aretino or of Dante Alighieri! Shaw says that good books should be excluded from library shelves so that people may be led to indulge their vices in reading, their virtues in life. If books could be a substitute for life this argument would not be specious. But since they are only guides to life it is important that they lead us not into temptation. The effect of books upon us is good if they guide us aright, evil if they lead us astray. But an evil book, however seductive, defeats itself as soon as we feel its venom, and its form cannot save it, being merely the vehicle of its meanness. If novels could be considered just in themselves they would be neither good nor bad; neither would they have any meaning. Students taking a course in the novel are likely to become bored with novels, whereas when they turn to one by way of relaxation from other courses they enjoy it. One who loses himself in novels, like the skipper in O'Brien's *White Shadows in the South Seas,* leaves them behind him evanescent as fading pipe dreams or the wake of a ship. Such a one is beyond boring because he is past appreciation, and he might as well eat opium. The value of novels is vicarious: it comes from life and refers back to it, as the charm of sea stories comes from the sea and in turn suffuses the sea with the sentiment of Conrad or Pierre Loti, and as the interest in love stories comes from love only to return to love more lovely than it came, so that real affection is finer than it could have been without fiction. Edna St. Vincent Millay says:

> Thus when I swear, "I love with all my heart,"
> 'Tis with the heart of Lilith that I swear,
> 'Tis with the love of Lesbia and Lucrece;
> And thus as well my love must lose some part
> Of what it is, had Helen been less fair,
> Or perished young, or stayed at home in Greece.

And again she says:

> With lovers such as we forevermore
> Isolde drinks the draught, and Guinevere
> Receives the Table's ruin through her door,
> Francesca, with the loud surf at her ear,
> Lets fall the colored book upon the floor.

Art always springs from an interest which is not originally aesthetic, and then transforms that interest with its own charm.

Coming back to bad books: they do represent values, but they exaggerate some to the detriment of others, which should not have been slighted. Such books may even do good in showing the reader the evil of over-cultivating a few interests at the expense of the integrity of personality. A bad book never has the power of a good one (over a balanced mind) because it appeals to only a part of the reader; badness in a book is partiality, limitation. It is often remarked that the very qualities which make some books bad are more forcefully represented in what are accepted as good books. These qualities make the other books bad because they were shown out of proportion. No values are bad in themselves, but only when represented out of perspective, and as soon as we recognize their distortion they lose any meretricious attraction they may momentarily have. As Milton says:

> Evil into the mind of God or Man
> May come and go, so unapproved, and leave
> No spot or blame behind.

We have to learn by experience what the true measure and balance is; we must check fiction by life, and recognize that it is good only as it helps toward a good life. Whatever is good for us is good, though perhaps we should take care not to cause our weak brother to stumble. Paul says if a man has faith he must have it in himself, before God; and "blessed is he who does not condemn himself in that which he discerns. But he who is in doubt, if he eats [or reads!], is condemned; because he does not eat with faith; and all that which is not of faith is sin." A censor only censors himself, for to the "impure" all things are pure and to the puritan sacred things may be tainted. What could be worse than parts of the

Old Testament when they fall into the hands of heathen puritans? Plato would surely have been horrified had they got into the mail of his ideal state. Yet the devout see no harm in them! As we grow in knowledge and the light of truth shines brighter, evil recedes like an unsubstantial shadow. Who is the villain in history whom a higher criticism will not whitewash? If Aretino had only had the advantages, the temptations—or whatever they were that the saints had which he lacked—if he could have played in their shining sandpiles and not have dirtied his hands making mud pies in the alley, we might not be righteously pointing our fingers at him today and calling him a bad boy. Why, he couldn't even read Greek and Latin, and his boasting that he never read books of any kind may have been just his way of covering up the fact that his education had been neglected and that he had no books in his house. As for his bullying, his bad manners, and his naughty language, don't they all show that he hadn't had a proper bringing up? He was just having a little fun by way of exuding his exuberance like any gamin who gets hailed into the juvenile court from the streets because he didn't have anyone to look after him or any back yard to play in. His very vices testify to his vitality, and with a little training they might quite conceivably have become virtues. He had the creative instinct and builded the best he could with mud, and whenever he wrought with something finer, as in his *Life of Christ,* the praise he got was that he probably stole it from one of his betters in the neighborhood. As for his chumming with Titian, instead of admiring his admiration for that good man, people said they just couldn't understand it, as if to imply that perhaps Titian was not so good or he would not have let him in the house. He was grateful for a little kindness, however, and never blackmailed Titian; but it was quite natural that he scourged the princes in return for their snubs, though that was not their fault since their mothers would not let them play with him, and though that was not really their mothers' fault either, since he always was a filthy rascal in seeming, however pink and white he may have been in his heart. Anyway, if we read him with some such understanding as this, what harm can he do us?

The only way of deciding between good and bad in literature is to consider what values are represented, and how well. Books which show us values in a more livable pattern than we had ever known them are inspiring; but those which fall short of our common life level cannot appeal to us. The more highly our lives are organized the more books there will be beneath us and the fewer above us, until some day perhaps we can say with Santayana that we read only the best authors and only their best works! But people who buy the latest fiction as they buy the latest haberdashery seem satisfied with any *Lebensanschauung,* so it be just off the press.

It is discontent, divine or not, restlessness, eagerness to get something more out of life which impels people to novels, and from ordinary ones to better ones. On the other hand, good novels often promote dissatisfaction with life as it is ordinarily lived. They then not only answer to an existent need, but awaken a new one. The power of problems to produce values is hardly greater than that of values to create problems. Desire makes an end desirable: sight of the end inflames desire. A youth's love will make any maid seem passing fair, but a lass who is surpassing fair will strike sparks from a heart of stone. Unfavorable circumstances make one dream of a better land, but a glimpse of heaven would cause discontent with the Garden of Eden. Misfortune always tends to arouse sympathy and tenderness, but when dramatized by a great tragedian and seen at the theater it will loosen the emotions even of those who are habitually unmoved. A boy naturally values athletic ability in his fellows, but when he sees an Olympic athlete his admiration is suddenly augmented by a glimpse of undreamed possibilities. Then he may see a statue by Myron of an ideal Olympic athlete, with the consequence that an appreciation of art is born, art which is the power to embody men's dreams as they had never hoped to see them. The boy's love for art will be akin to his old liking for athletes, but it will be something higher, a desire which can no longer be satisfied by natural forms, but only by the ideal shapes of the sculptor, and not even by them, for the highest art points upward to forms it cannot attain, and when one has once been drawn to contemplation of these divine essences, a longing is awakened which nothing on earth can allay. Then one wonders whether the original stimulus was a push from a problem which projected the ideal of its own solution, or a pull from an ideal which threw back the problem of its attainment. Such an ultimate question is perhaps unanswerable. This we know: that, as we know them, problems do push, and ideals do pull. Problems run up values like flags on a battleship, and values suck problems after them like whirlpools. Sometimes the wish is father to the thought, and sometimes it is the other way. Hunger will arouse the idea of food, and the idea will increase the hunger, whereupon the hunger will strengthen the idea. If a vague velleity causes a hazy idea of its satisfaction, the idea will tend to make the velleity a definite desire, which in turn may make what was a passing fancy a fixed obsession. If the wish fathers a thought, the thought fosters the wish, and there is no stopping this side of Paradise.

Literature, then, is not simply a refuge and a shelter, but a challenge. Much as it is valued as a solace and a comfort to those who are weary and are heavy laden, as a spice to those who are sleek and surfeited, it is more valuable as a *reveillé* to those who are ready for a new vision, a newly awakened life on a higher level. Shelley said: "Poets are the trumpets which sing to battle, poets are the unacknowledged legislators of the world."

V

WHAT PERSONALITY IS

Novels help people to see what they are groping and yearning for. They show them their dreams better than they could dream them; they open new vistas to their imagination. They enable them better to see themselves and others, and what they may become. In the novel men see society as in a glass, its future as in a crystal. It lets them look into the eyes of their own souls, feel again the poignancy of childhood, and foretaste the regret and resignation of age. Infancy, childhood, adolescence, senescence—the whole of life is there, passing before the fancy with a beginning, a rising, a falling, chapter following chapter, unrolling the life of man, whose history is a story, whose days are as many pages printed and bound in a volume, a book that is held in the hand. Fate is no longer writ on the dark scroll of the sky charactered with stars, but on fair sibylline leaves, less white for the meaning they bear, the meaning of life and of death, of earth and of heaven. All is written there as fast as the oracle speaks, and the most precious leaves, those most beautifully lettered, those most tenderly treasured, tell of the spirit of man, his birth and rebirth and salvation.

Literature has the advantage of science in representing human life more directly and in its own terms. Science speaks in symbols and formulas foreign to current discourse, because it tries to escape the ordinary human point of view and see the world "as it is." But literature is concerned with representing the world only as it appears to men in their different moods and emotions, through the medium of language familiar to the heart, instead of through a technical vocabulary consciously avoiding emotive associations. In literature language is not strained to render to our thought things as they may be outside our thought, but thoughts are rendered literally by thoughts, discourse is represented by discourse, so that ideas stand simply for ideas, which, according to Berkeley, is all that they can legitimately stand for. It is said that Berkeley's early devotion to airy romance explains his antipathy to matter and his zeal for proving that the ideal alone is real. He did at least prove that for the human mind the world is as it appears. Thus the most aerial romance, if it express an emotion true of experience, is absolutely real; whereas a materialistic statement of matter must go beyond our experience and therefore seem unreal to us. But modern science is etherealizing matter until it is akin to our own spirit, until as a matter of fact there is no longer a fact of matter. Matter is a fiction, wherefore the foundation of literature, instead of being undermined by science, is reaffirmed. Facts are fictitious, and fiction alone is factual; science is a department of literature, of the expression of the human spirit. That is to say that science is literally true only in so far as it is literature, in so far as it renders life in its historical individuality and particularity. But science for its practical purpose must abstract and generalize, whereas literature for its aesthetic purpose must never sacrifice the bright vitality of life to a stolid statement about it; it is a close-up view of life's values. The novel is now the dominant form of literature because it is most capable of binding in one cover the significance of the individual as a person and of society as a whole.

The main thing in the novel, as in life which it represents, is the point of view, the attitude. Thus the young Shakespeare, while a butcher-boy, would make a speech and ceremony over killing a pig. There is nothing in a calling, but everything in a man's response to his vocation: one will make an art of his trade, another will make a trade of his art, as the Sophist did. The chief concern of every man, after health, is to see his life in such a way that he can enter into it with zest. Stevenson confesses that as a child he could not bring himself to study his alphabet except by imagining himself a business man at his desk. Some men keep going all their lives by thinking of themselves as business men, chafing when kept away from the office, and not dreaming of retirement. Stevenson, when older, kept heart through the most discouraging conditions by thinking of himself as a man of letters. It makes little difference what the rôle be, so it interest a man enough to call out the best that is in him. Keeping a store, or anything that is fun as play, may continue to absorb a man so long as he maintains the attitude of play.

Once a rôle has seized a man's imagination he will gladly do everything he conceives to belong to the part, as the young artist will undergo, and even seek, the hardship of the garret. Don Quixote is the personification of every man playing a part, getting up and carrying on with it though unhorsed and ridiculed, welcoming everything that belongs to the rôle, reading the books about it, and conscientiously working into the character the interpretations of the greatest actors. Aside from compulsion, a child accomplishes things only through the play interest, and this is equally true of an adult. The men who have done the most work often feel that they have never done any work, because to them it was all play. Unfortunately most men have to work from necessity; but in so far as this is true, their interest is external to their work. It does not seem fair that those who have the most uninspiring parts in the world's work are usually those with the least imagination for dramatizing them, while those with the most absorbing rôles are those with the greatest ability to see significance in their efforts. On the other hand, easy circumstances are often harder on sensitive, imaginative souls than hard circumstances on the insensitive, for imagination may be a curse as well as a blessing. At any rate some degree of play interest is necessary to make work seem worth while. Tom Sawyer discovered that even drudgery will be done eagerly when infused with fun. The attraction of religion is largely due to its immense aid in dramatizing life through its calendar, ritual, and pageantry, with its host of ideal characters to keep one company through tedium. This is also the mission of literature: to provide the soul with society, and interpret life interestingly. For life to be endurable its misery must contribute to its glory; its joy must be exalted, and its sorrow made dramatically subordinate thereto; its suffering must be transmuted into rejoicing, as the bitter cross is made the sweet sign of redemption.

Life is likely to be uninteresting unless one can make play of it. While it is a fine thing for tradespeople to serve their fellows, they will take small pleasure in that unless they get some fun out of it, and the same is true of professional men, scientists, artists, and philosophers. A youth who has not decided what he wants to do in the world is prone to be very unhappy, for he has no part in the drama of life and he cannot quite share in the zest of it until he has one. He envies the tailor with his big shears, the locomotive engineer pulling his levers, the smart bank clerk with his quick fingers, even the elevator boy and the janitor. He envies them, not because they are helping the world along nor because they are earning their living, but because they have parts in the cast of life, while he is without one, has no character. For a time he had had one: as a child in school, as a student in high school and college, but wish as he will that he had that rôle back, it is gone from him. There are cynics who take pride in having no part, but a normal person wants to get into the play, and when he gets an opportunity he studies his part and rehearses it with gusto. James remarks how quickly the professional manner settles upon a man, and it is no wonder: for if he wants to be a doctor or a lawyer, a butcher or baker, he will adopt as speedily as possible the appropriate air in order to convince himself as well as others that he is really playing the part. It is by pretending to be grown up that we finally grow up, by assuming confidence that we become confident, and it is by taking a rôle that we really become a person.

We all act parts: we feel happy when we play up to the rôle we imagine for ourselves, and humiliated when we slip into deeds or words that are out of character. We are born actors, good or bad, and all believe that the play's the thing. While apparently some parts are preferable to others, we have much of the Stoic feeling that it matters little what part is assigned us, but much how we carry it off. We are bored by people without character more than by people with a character that does not appeal to us, for it is possible for any character to be remarkable if it is well acted. But people without any "characteristic" to distinguish them merely clutter up the stage or swell the chorus, for they arouse no expectation of any kind, and consequently never give us aesthetic pleasure in fulfilling it, or even displeasure in failing to do so. We like to be able to say of a person that "that" was just like him, that we might have known he'd do "it," since "it" was himself all over. Nothing can make up for lack of character in this aesthetic sense of fidelity to a part, whatever it may be. If energy and alacrity be his dramatic motive, as in the case of D'Artagnan, that is what we require of him and delight in when he appears; if it be laziness and stupidity, as in the case of the fat boy in Pickwick, that is what we demand and enjoy when he comes on. What we ask of a person in the play of life is that he give a dominant note and then improvise in harmony with it. If he's going to be as solemn as a judge, all right, only woe to him if he unbend when he thinks no one is looking. If he's going to be as funny as a clown, all right, but woe to him if he sober up. Let him be a saint if he can, or a sinner if he can; let him be a real one, and his place in the human drama is secure. Whether he be magnanimous or petty, immaculate or spotted, it will be accepted, so he keep it up and carry it off to the final curtain.

For illustration of this we naturally turn to history, where the great characters of all time are on parade, or to fiction, where the undated characters of the imagination dwell. The great ones of history have struggled free from the inconsistencies and irrelevancies that clouded their actual performance, while the great ones of story were born free to be themselves from their creators' brains. To them we turn in despair of finding real characters in the life about us, though now and then we do find them, with a pang of surprise, sometimes in fine houses, more often in the street. More than most, a beggar is likely to be a character, wherefore Dorothy Richardson says she does not pity him, she thanks God for him. He must put his whole heart into his rôle in order to succeed at all, whereas most of us can get by on a relatively half-hearted interpretation of an easier part, and that tends to dilute the color of our personality. A teacher or a preacher or a storekeeper or a clerk who does not entirely like his vocation tries to avoid a speech and manner indicative of his calling, and thereby loses his distinction. But if a man is going to be a beggar he has to appear to be an honest-to-goodness one; he has to look and talk the part; he has to be positive; he is forced to be a person; while the man he begs from, for all he may have his name in the telephone book, is only a man in the street. It does not follow that we should all become mendicant, nor that we should take up some bizarre pursuit. If only we could be content to be really ourselves we should not be tempted to become freaks. Yet in the delusion that individuality is the same as eccentricity we have nearly reached the point where it is abnormal to be normal: it is now so conventional to be unconventional that the only way to be unconventional is to be conventional.

It is difficult, however, to know what it means "to be one's self." If it were a matter of picking out one rôle and sticking to it, it would be relatively simple, but that is nearly impossible for most of us. Neither the *poseur* nor the plain man is exclusively absorbed in a single rôle. No one part completely satisfies anyone, and if it did the world would still compel one to alternate with other rôles now and then, as a grand opera company does. Then, in addition to having different major parts, there are a multitude of minor ones which one chooses or is thrust into by all the little acts and accidents of the day. One may have to take the cook's place, the janitor's, the gardener's. A complete personality includes many interests, each one of which in itself might theoretically or practically constitute a character. Then people constantly appropriate attitudes and mannerisms from each other. Conspicuous characters in life, in fiction, and on the stage so stamp certain acts or expressions as their own that through them we enter into their rôles. Hence the analysis of a self is often as startling as the examination of a vaudeville swallower's stomach containing quantities of pins, nails, tacks, and other unsuspected articles. The story of Dr. Jekyll and Mr. Hyde is far from the truth, for it is incredible that there should be only two persons resident in one man. For instance, the inventory of the selves a man has just from his reading would be something like this:

When he reads Dumas he is Stevenson; when he cashes a check he is D'Artagnan in the presence of Colbert; when he endeavors to write something he is the elegant Aramis trying to write his thesis; when he is in love with an older girl he is Shakespeare; when he is in love with a child he is Poe, or Verlaine, or Dowson; when he is in love with a mature woman he is the youth in *The Dark Flower;* when he has indigestion he is William James; when he reads the Bible he is Robinson Crusoe; when he reads Robinson Crusoe he is the old steward in "The Moonstone"; when he reads of knight-errantry he is Don Quixote, or Cervantes himself; when he reads Don Quixote he is Immanuel Kant refreshing himself from his labor on *Die Kritik der Reinen Vernunft;* when he reads Kant he is the Opium Eater; when he reads aloud he is De Quincey or Swinburne; when he takes a long walk he is Swinburne or Dickens; when he runs he is Sassoon; when he skates he is Goethe; when he swims he is Byron; when he sails he is Shelley; when he plays cards he is Dostoievsky in *The House of the Dead;* when he reads in bed he is Jack London; when he spends the forenoon writing letters he is Madame Merle, the worldly woman in *The Portrait of a Lady;* when he airs a suit in the sun he is Yann in *Pêcheur d'Islande,* who learned such attentions aboard a battleship; when he shaves he is the old sailor in *The Rescue;* when he does not shave he is Joseph Conrad; when he studies day and night he is the Chevalier des Grieux in the Seminary of Saint-Sulpice; when he takes exercise he is Edmond Dantès in the Château d'If—and when he is just himself he is nobody.

There is nothing more disconcerting than the admonition to be one's self. When one is just one's self one's self vanishes, because the self is nothing apart from the other selves it has taken in. One has no self to begin with; the self is not an endowment, but an achievement of appropriating the selves of others, taking inside the society that surrounds one, holding a salon in the mind. After talking with others and taking over their rôles, the child is able to talk with himself. The infant has no self until, through intercourse with others, he begins to respond to his own stimuli in the same way that they do, and so puts himself in their place and makes their personalities his own. Conversation develops when gestures mean the same to him who makes them as to the others; that is, when each realizes the significance of the stimuli he gives by responding to them himself. In no other way can he put himself in another's place and be able to talk with him. In this way the child soon learns how to approach different people and wheedle them; by putting himself in their places and taking over their rôles he learns what will appeal to them. The tactful child or person is the one who is most successful in taking the point of view of others, who avoids awkwardness with them by checking inappropriate gestures in their incipiency, because he responds to them as the other would and ahead of the other, thus enabling himself to modulate and adjust his conduct to their satisfaction. For this reason he can tell as much about another person by the kind of things he is prompted to say or write to him as by the replies he gets from him. He rarely addresses a person in a language he will not understand or in a tone he will resent, unless deliberately trying to mystify or offend him. He even talks baby-talk to a baby and slips into the accent of a foreigner. With different people he is himself a different person, so that it would be very embarrassing to invite all his friends to the same party. The self is social; it is constituted by the selves with which one has intercourse, and could not arise in solitude, though it may seemingly maintain itself apart from society after it has been developed therein, because the society which initially had been external to it is now contained within it. A person is able to talk with himself, that is, to think, when he has taken over the rôles of different persons which may then hold forth in his own inner forum. When he thinks, there are at least two interlocutors within him. A child cannot think until he has taken in at least one self to stand over against his self and draw it out. For his own self, like a genii, appears when another self has uncorked it, and shrinks again into insignificance when that other goes away. There cannot be just one self in isolation any more than there can be only one pole of electricity. As Professor Mead says, a self is that which can be a self to itself. The social character of the self is evident in reflection when different protagonists adopt different points of view within the same person. Dreaming is another example. We are never alone in a dream:

CARL A. RUDISILL LIBRARY
LENOIR RHYNE COLLEGE

the several personalities which constitute each one of us, which in thought are often merely voices in a dialogue, in a dream are embodied in forms and we feel identified with all of them, as if we were the many persons at once which we really are.

Mere multiplicity of selves, however, is not enough to make a complete self: there must also be a continual development through the acquisition of new selves. When we have learned the rôles of those about us and they have learned ours, the flow of stimulus and response tends to reach a dead level when the tide no longer rises and falls in the bays of our own souls because it has ceased in the outer sea of intercourse. There is no profit in talking with others when we and they both know what will be said before it is spoken; and there is no incentive to talk with ourselves when there are no fresh aspects within. We have no self of our own before we have brought in other selves, and we begin to lose it when those others are thoroughly absorbed in us. Disillusion comes from reducing the fresh new life about us to the original non-being of our own dark spirit, which was enlivened by the selves taken into it, only to seem blacker after using up their light. Such utter self-absorption and stagnation, however, rarely overtakes men, because they cannot stir about the world at all without having the spark within fanned by the influence of others.

One is constantly obliged to make readjustments, to modify attitudes, take new perspectives; and everyone brightens up with a change of rôle, as the child is refreshed by playing the parent because it is a relief from being a child. It is dull to be one's self all the time. It is exhilarating to be someone else, especially someone unusual or removed from our own plane so as not to be too easily domesticated and made part of our tame self—one whom we cannot keep in our own back yard, but will rather lead us clear out of our little bailiwick. Thus we like to act in a rôle which envelopes our commonplace self in a cloak of romance in which we can overstep the flat circle of familiarity. We like to do things with style, like Tom Sawyer, for things please us in others, and in ourselves, when they are done with imagination, with character—that is, *in character*. A thing amounts to something when done thus, and the one who does it thereby becomes somebody because he becomes somebody else. This gives curve and cut to life and makes it zestful, because it makes us self-conscious. While it is a fine thing to live at all, compared to being a stock or a stone, it is foolish not to enjoy the most lively life available, that of self-consciousness.

Plain ordinary consciousness comes with a check upon habitual activity, involving a sharpening of attention, a heightening of emotion, and a scurry of the organism to get out of difficulty. All the animals must have this kind of consciousness, more or less, which comes and goes as they get into scrapes and out again; yet here is no self other than the empty Kantian ego of apperceptive unity. *Self*-consciousness is reserved to man, for he is the only creature, so far as we are aware, who is able to acquire a self which can be a self to itself. An ant returning with food indicates to the other ants that there is food about, and they troop after it because they have noticed him with it, but the informing ant apparently does not know that he is indicating anything to the others. Man, however, can treat himself as another and point out to himself what he shows to others, and thereby be conscious of himself and what he is doing, because, having the rôles of others within him, he can look at himself through their eyes. Since each man says to himself what he is saying to the other, he knows just what he is saying. Men respond inwardly to the stimuli they give outwardly; thus each of them builds up the self of the other within his own self, so that when that self is fully developed there is as much society within it as without. In short, as Professor Mead says, a man may call on himself and find himself at home.

Yet he must keep renewing his acquaintance with his self or it will tend to disappear, for it is impossible to remain aware of what is become completely familiar. The faces of our closest friends are likely to be indistinct to us, and we make the same errors in recalling them as we do in describing the faces of our watches, because they are habitual to us, part of us, tucked away in a pocket of our consciousness; whereas we may clearly remember a face or a watch which we have seen only once. We know our friend so well that we do not need to think what he looks like. In the beginning we saw him clearly; thereafter we saw him just well enough to recognize him and make sure of his presence; and now perhaps we notice no more than a familiar gesture or the tone of voice indissolubly associated with him—just enough to give us the cue for the response we have ready for him, the name we call him by, the things we have to say to him, and to keep from him. In meeting someone we know only slightly we are much more observant and cautious; not one, but several cues must be received before we risk a response, including height, hat, coat, complexion, and features, which we would not examine in an old friend any more than we would study the letters in a familiar word. Our increased consciousness of the appearance of strangers reacts upon ourselves, making us self-conscious, and we are embarrassed or flattered according to the figure we seem to cut in their eyes; we are stimulated to show off in an effort to attract the approbation we are denied in the intimate circle of family and close friends, where anything we do is taken for granted as much as our hair and eyes and whole accepted self. On the other hand we are secretly more eager to impress familiars than strangers, because that is a greater triumph. Strangers may be too easily taken in, since to them our most threadbare and mechanical accomplishments may be novel and wonderful; or strangers may be too difficult and skeptical to estimate us, discounting our fresh, newly won attainments, thinking they are just part of our stock in trade. Thus only our familiars are qualified to judge us after all. Before the world we are all like the members of circus families: the spectators gape or yawn according to the spectacularity of our feats; we take their money and bow to their applause, or ignore their ridicule, but the praise or blame which heals or hurts is strictly *en famille*. The self we are conscious of in the presence of outsiders is a kind of Sunday self, with special manners and "company" voice; let the world turn and tear it, we are safe until betrayed by our bosom friends—then, like Brutus, we are undone.

Self-consciousness is man's special possession, the cause of his joy and his grief. What he lives for is his picture of himself, and if his life make it hideous it will kill him as it did Dorian Gray. Primitive man keeps conscious of himself by painting and tattooing his body, decking it with ornaments to show what a fine fellow he is, with trophies to show what a fierce fellow he is. The social nature of his most intimate self he often symbolizes by fusing his blood with that of another and trading names with him, that each may become the other. Modern man would rather display himself through works of his hand or mind, and decorate his wife; but he too craves the recognition of the many and finds satisfaction only in the response of a few. He cannot bear a situation in which no response is personally accorded him. Men are content to wear uniform clothing in civil life, where they may have individuality, but they chafe under it in prison or in the army, where the uniform connotes uniformity of personality. Woman, as she gains freedom to develop herself, is less dependent upon raiment for self-consciousness and is more content to dress like others when she can remind herself in more subtle ways that she is different; but the woman who still fails to develop individuality in other ways is more anxious than ever to dress strikingly. The changing fashions even in men's clothing, however, indicate a perennial search for self-consciousness through external means. A mysterious person in Paris or London could not make people jump out of one costume into another like the director of a stage troupe if we were not stage people, ever bent upon playing a new rôle and looking a new part. Some do defy the director with a velvet jacket or a white suit, like Stevenson or Mark Twain, but the opportunity for individuality through dress is relatively restricted. Our individual garb is hardly more distinctive than that of savages, but it is possible for our thought to be infinitely varied. W. H. Hudson observed that the children of Indian tribes seemed old while they were still young because it took only a few years for them to learn all the adult adjustments to life; whereas in our society there is so much to learn that one who tries to learn it can almost never grow up.[1]

Children are a joy because they are growing and changing all the time, have so much hope ahead and so little regret behind, and because while they are mastering the parts of their parents, teachers, and friends, these in turn are learning the bright new rôles of the children. The world is more interesting every year through the new children coming into it and because the grown-ups themselves must be more and more like children in the increasing difficulty of attaining a final adjustment to a changing world.

It is said that when two men have to spend a whole winter together in the frozen north they are likely to come to loathe each other, because each acquires the entire rôle of the other and then has to keep on pretend-

[1] "Guter Gott von deinem Himmel! Alte Kinder siehst du und junge Kinder, und nichts weiter; und an welchen du mehr Freude hast, das hat dein Sohn schon lange verkündigt."—GOETHE.

ing that there are two persons present, after the personality has gone out of each into the other and disappeared. In a longer time three or four men might so reduce each other, though this would not be so apt to happen as in a dual relationship—yet let something go wrong, let all brood upon the same disappointment or hardship, and four may melt into one, so that each sees in the others nothing but a dark reflection of himself. This tends to happen in any family too much shut in upon itself, where each sees his faults and virtues in the others until he fears to lose his identity. Keyserling speaks of the banality of life on shipboard due to the herding together which reduces all the passengers to the same psychic level. The backwardness of any isolated community comes from the same thing. Self-consciousness depends upon the conquest of other selves; and when those other selves are completely subdued it disappears. Perhaps self-consciousness does not completely vanish, or there would be no bitterness about it, or any other sentiment—only the external give and take of animal relations. The maddening thing is to see the human features of those with whom we are herded too closely gradually become transmogrified into the brutish, to feel that their humanity, their selfhood, is slipping, and our own simultaneously, until, as if under the influence of Circe's wand, the eyes of our companions look small and intent like those of monkeys, their downy ears look like the furry ones of squirrels, and their attitudes at table remind us of "an omnivorous mammal having a long mobile snout with flat expanded end containing the nostrils."

A child might break the spell; a visitor would; a book could go a long way; but in primitive and out-of-the-way places what has saved humanity has been work, especially where it involved social intercourse, as well as war and play. Man has built up his selfhood by taking over the selves of others, and whenever he could not come in contact with outsiders he has sought self-realization at home, where it cannot be found, because there each steals what the other has of personality until there is none left. Hence civil and domestic discord arise when there are no warlike or peaceful diversions abroad, and if isolation continue long enough, human nature falls away, leaving nothing but nature. Isolated groups degenerate quite as much from social as from physical inbreeding. The group must be ventilated by foreign influences. A child, as long as he is learning the rôles of his parents, and they his, will agitate the atmosphere; but when he reaches their limit they touch his, and there is no longer a child between them. Yet if the personality of each is continually recharged from without, the child cannot overtake his parents nor they him.

Modern facilities in travel and communication bid fair to prevent anyone going stale anywhere, all the novelty from the ends of the earth being deposited daily on each breakfast table—or will freshness and strangeness thereby be destroyed, distance and illusion disappear, and individuality be lost? There might be this gloomy ending in store after millions of years if there were any limit to the novelty of the world; but there is certainly no such end in sight. Rather, science is teaching us that life continually rises to new levels where fresh values emerge which could not have been predicted or imagined from a lower stage. No analysis of the inorganic world would ever reveal that a different synthesis of the same elements would produce organisms; no study of the lowest life would suggest that a later organization of the same cells would produce such activities as running and climbing, and eventually thinking, dreaming, and praying. No introspection on the part of a child could intimate the possibilities life has in store for him. Thus Virginia Woolf's Mrs. Dalloway said to Rachel: "When you're my age you'll see that the world is *crammed* with delightful things. I think young people make such a mistake about that."[2]

Multiplicity and diversity of selves make personality, much as many different cells make the body. There cannot be a self until there are several selves in one; and a self cannot continue if the many completely coalesce into one. On the one hand this coalescence is dreaded and avoided as the death of individuality; on the other hand this death is sought by some as the birth of a new life beyond selfhood, in which the creature merges again with the creator. Most people in the Western world want to be conspicuously different, though they dare not think or dress except with such inconspicuous individuality that no one would notice their difference; yet a child like the Little Flower of Lisieux seeks oblivion and yearns for obscurity, and St. Peter's flares with lights in her honor.

Most people, however, desire to be personal. Perhaps the greatest aid to personality is the dichotomy of

[2] *The Voyage Out*, p. 58.

the race into sexes forever curious about each other. It is likely that a man and woman alone in the wilderness could safely preserve their identities longer than two normal people of the same sex. But even the fascination of sex will fail with too much familiarity. Eugene O'Neill, in *Ile,* shows how a wife goes stark mad after two years on a whaling trip when return to civilization is delayed. For one person to keep his personality all alone for a long period is most difficult. The precautions of Robinson Crusoe to remind himself of his self show how much he was in fear of losing it. He cut notches on a post for a calendar, read his Bible daily, kept a diary with diluted ink, cherished his dog and his cat as himself, and welcomed Friday to the palisade as the salvation of his soul. He was lucky in being left a shipload of supplies, not only for their material aid, but because of the associations they established with his larger self. This good fortune may have made the difference between his consciousness of self and the absence of it in Ben Gunn marooned on Treasure Island, and the wild man of Tabor Island, described in *The Mysterious Island* of Jules Verne.

Those hermits who succeeded in retaining their self-consciousness and humanity acquired it originally through commerce with others and kept it by continuing that intercourse in imagination, often with the help of books, and always with the ideal companionship of the saints. It is doubtful, however, whether a hermetically isolated hermit could stay human indefinitely, inasmuch as the repertory of rôles he began with would eventually be learned by rote, and he would so absorb and confuse them that he could no longer oppose one to the other, or if he could continue to do so at all the process would become so habitual and automatic that he would not be conscious of it. Books would be his only hope; but since books get their meaning from society, it is unlikely that a man entirely cut off from his fellows would continue to find significance in them, just as we cannot appreciate books of other cultures except in so far as we are able to come in contact with them. Great as the difficulty would be of keeping a personality intact in isolation, it would be impossible for an infant left alone with the beasts of the jungle, like Tarzan of the Apes, to build up a human self. It took the whole race of man long ages to bring human nature into the world, and it takes the race as a whole to keep it alive. A human self cannot exist in a limited group; and today any group is limited which is not open to the whole past, present, and future of man.

A personality is constituted by a plurality of selves. To stay plural the selves must be too diverse to merge, and to stay diverse they must be continually recruited from without. That is why we want to grow up, to get away from home, to make new friends, and to read new novels. And that is why we are also tenderly attached to our childhood, our home, our old friends, and old books. We want new experience, but it always makes us appreciate the security of the old. Home does not mean so much to the son who stays there as to the prodigal. When we are shut in the house we look wistfully out of the window at the passers-by, while perhaps they look longingly in. Yet if it is romantic to encounter adventure abroad, it is grateful to return to the castle and lay aside our armor. It is after being outside that we most enjoy the fireside. Sir Thomas More feeding the birds at Chelsea is the picture of domestic felicity because we see him enjoying a brief respite from the unquiet court of Henry VIII.

Old friends are a part of home, and we really appreciate them also after we have left them. To part from those who have become as habitual to us as the garments we wear is difficult, for, though we may have been barely aware of them these many years, the separation makes us poignantly conscious of each other and of ourselves. Our old homes and friends gain new charm when we leave them because, while they are part of ourselves, the leavetaking puts them in such perspective that we no longer overlook them as we do our own person and immediate surroundings; it puts them again on the level of our vision, where they were when they first appeared on our horizon, where we can keep them in easy focus and enjoy watching them as we watch ships on the skyline. Stevenson has expressed this in a letter from Vailima to Sidney Colvin:

> Though I write so little, I pass all my hours of field work in continual converse and imaginary correspondence. I scarce pull up a weed but I invent a sentence on the matter to yourself; it does not get written; *autant emportent les vents;* but the intent is there, and for me (in some sort) the companionship. Today, for instance, we had a great talk. . . . . And take my life all through, look at it fore and back, and upside down—though I would very fain change myself—I would not change my circumstances, unless it were to bring you here. And yet God knows perhaps this inter-

> course of writing serves as well; and I wonder, were you here indeed, would I commune so continually with the thought of you. I say "I wonder" for a form; I know, and I know I should not.[3]

Walter Pater says, "One builds up from act and word and expression of the friend actually visible at one's side, an ideal of the spirit within him,"[4] and when the friend is out of sight his spirit is not less real in our mind, but rather more so for the loss of his physical presence. That loss is none the less a loss, however, for we long for contact, and when reunion is possible it is as poignant as parting, because it again renders us suddenly and overwhelmingly conscious of ourselves. The union of new acquaintances is cautious and reserved, but the reunion of old friends is like the confluence of divided waters.

Childhood, like home and old friends, is also regretted when it is gone. The child wants to play the parent and to grow up, but the parent would gladly play the child and be young. It is evidently uninteresting to be a child all the time, while it is fun to pretend to be a grown man and to dream of the time when one will be one. Yet it is also quite commonplace to be grown up, compared to having been a child. Personality reaches up toward the adult world and then yearns backward, like those vines which strike root again in the soil they have left. Stevenson explains Pepys's *Diary* by the love he had for his former self. When he saw how it was slipping from him he not only tried to recall it, but came to see his actual self from the point of view of his future self,

[3] *Letters,* III, 288, 289.

[4] *Marius the Epicurean* (Modern Library edition), p. 254.

and, as it were, wrote letters to that coming self. Stevenson notes that we all do this when we inscribe in our books when and where we read them. Stevenson's own affection for the child he had been is of course expressed in *A Child's Garden of Verse*. *Le Livre de Mon Ami* of Anatole France is one of the tenderest recollections of childhood which novelists have left us,[5] and *A la Recherche du Temps Perdu*, by Marcel Proust, is the most marvelous.

"But in every one of us," says William James, "there are moments when this complete reproduction of all the items of past experience occurs. What are those moments? They are moments of emotional recall of the past as something which once was, but is gone forever—moments the interest of which consists in the feeling that our self was once other than it now is. When this is the case, any detail, however minute, which will make

[5] "Je vais vous dire ce que me rappellent, tous les ans, le ciel agité de l'automne, les premiers dîners à la lampe, et les feuilles qui jaunissent dans les arbres qui frissonnent; je vais vous dire ce que je vois quand je traverse le Luxembourg dans les premiers jours d'octobre, alors qu'il est un peu triste et plus beau que jamais; car c'est le temps où les feuilles tombent une à une sur les blanches épaules des statues. Ce que je vois alors dans ce jardin, c'est un petit bonhomme qui, les mains dans les poches et sa gibecière au dos, s'en va au collège en sautillant comme un moineau. Ma pensée seule le voit; car ce petit bonhomme est une ombre; c'est l'ombre du *moi* que j'étais il y a vingt-cinq ans. Vraiment il m'intéresse, ce petit; quand il existait, je ne me souciais guère de lui; mais, maintenant qu'il n'est plus, je l'aime bien. Il valait mieux, en somme, que les autres *moi* que j'ai eus après avoir perdu celui-là. Il était bien étourdi; mais il n'était pas méchant et je dois lui rendre cette justice qu'il ne m'a pas laissé un seul mauvais souvenir; c'est un innocent que j'ai perdu: il est bien naturel que je le regrette; il est bien naturel que je le voie en pensée et que mon esprit s'amuse à ranimer son souvenir" (Henry Holt edition, p. 101).

the past picture more complete will also have its effect in swelling that total contrast between *now* and *then* which forms the central interest of our contemplation."[6]

Today analogous interest is developed in the childhood of the race: we have the same sentiment for our prehistoric selves that we have for the selves of our infancy and school days; and, like Pepys, we are thereby made conscious of our present period and impelled to record it for the sake of our future selves in coming centuries. Self-consciousness seems to be the chief end of man; without it he has no self; without it he is not man. He achieves it by putting himself in the place of others and making their selves part of his own; and this conquest of foreign selves is not complete until they are organized into an inner empire. After the acquisition of many parts a man's main problem is his title-rôle, his personality *par excellence*, which is to govern his minor characteristics and make a unity of his many selves which he can call *himself*. A personality not only contains many rôles, suited to intercourse with various persons and to action in many diverse situations, but it also gives a distinctive interpretation to all these rôles, as a closet containing many different dresses will scent them all with the same perfume. A point of view giving a peculiar perspective, enabling one to see the world as no other does, is the essence of personality or self-consciousness.

By self-consciousness is not meant the state of blushing embarrassment. The discomfort of this condition is caused by the sudden dissolution of the self: we

[6] *The Principles of Psychology*, I, 571.

do something which we will not own to be characteristic of us, we push it away, declaring that in doing it we were not ourself, and then either smooth it over to fit our real self, or try to forget it. As long as embarrassment or remorse continues, we are not conscious of being ourself, but of not being ourself. If we do have to admit that the act was part of us we say it was our evil self and not our good or real self; and in that case we are aware, not of a self, but of selves too divergent to merge. Diversity of selves is necessary to the self, but if they become too disparate the self is disrupted. The two men in the wilderness, whom we assumed to hate each other because their selves coalesced, would have hated each other much sooner had a marked dissidence in their selves precluded congeniality. The manifold selves within a personality are always in danger either of utterly taming each other so that there ceases to be interaction among them, or of so antagonizing each other that no reconciliation is possible—in either case personality being destroyed, for while it must have both heterogeneity and homogeneity, an excess of either is fatal.

The effort of each person is to get a lively company of selves and to keep them congenial by having them all join together in a unified plan of life. This endeavor to have many selves which shall fit into one self is the great preoccupation, and each is on the lookout for helpful hints and suggestions. Those who have achieved the most interesting personalities are objects of universal attention: they are the leaders in the quest for self-consciousness, and foremost among them are the novelists.

Personality, aside from its importance to the individual as his own consciousness of self, has a wider significance as the growing-point of society. The institutions and customs, the universals of society, are made over in the individual. "So treated," says Mr. Dewey, "they are tentative, dubious, but experimental anticipations of an object. They are 'subjective' (i.e., individualistic) surrogates of public, cosmic things, which may be so manipulated and elaborated as to terminate in public things which without them would not exist as empirical objects."[7] These universals which operate impersonally and at large in society are called into court only in the minds of individuals; there they are questioned and made to square up with each other. As the self develops by taking over the attitudes and responses of its milieu it becomes aware of discrepancies and shortcomings among them. To maintain its identity and hold together as a self it must make an adjustment which is both a reflection of public things as they are and an anticipation of them as they may be reconstructed. The self is not a self until it has taken in other selves; moreover, it is not entirely established until these other selves are organized into what Professor Mead calls the "generalized other," or the organization of society as a whole over against the individual. By becoming a person one undertakes to live with the generalized other. A person cannot escape it without ceasing to be himself, for it is himself in relation to society. It is not only his self, but that of every other member as well. Society at large

[7] *Essays in Experimental Logic*, p. 228.

lodged within the individual is the generalized other. Mr. Mead uses games in illustration of this.

A boy cannot really play any position on a ball team until he has built up within himself an appreciation of all the other positions. To be a first-baseman he must be able to put himself in the place of the pitcher, the batter, the men on bases, the fielders, etc.; he must know what each of the others is expected to do at each juncture of the game in order to know what is expected of himself. He must guide and check each of his movements in accordance with the generalized other which he has built up within himself through his experience of the rôles of the others. In any social group one's success or failure depends upon ability to organize one's responses in harmony with the generalized other. The tactful, successful person responds to his own incipient movements before the others are aware of them, and represses those which might offend. He puts himself in their place, he spares their feelings, and chimes in with their mood, because by having built up their selves within himself he has only to consult his own feelings to know how to behave. Such a person gets along with everyone because he is everyone in turn, man and woman and child, because he is gay or sad, fresh or fatigued, in a sufficient degree to sympathize with his friends at every turn, and thus know exactly what each situation demands of him, like a good ball-player.

As some people can play only one or two games, so there are those who can get along in only a few groups, outside of which they are nervous and awkward. Allowing for degrees of native ability, experience makes the difference between the yokel who is at home on a keg before the country store, the cosmopolite who is at ease in any company in the world, and the philosopher who haunts all time and existence. A man's personality is measured by the scope of society which he has absorbed and generalized within himself. His caliber is gauged by the angle of society which he subtends. But the generalized other of society at large is always greater than any individual. It is the social self of the race; it is man living in men. One learns more of it as one's personality develops and becomes more social; but to no man has it been fully revealed, nor is it glimpsed alike by all. Yet whatever men share through association they have in common through the generalized other.

Our relations with it are not fixed, because it is not fixed, nor are we. It was here ahead of any of us, and as we grow we become acquainted with its manifoldness. Yet as we develop each of us affects each other so that the generalized other itself is modified. Each of us introduces some novelty into society, though none of us alone can remake it, nor all of us together, overnight. The generalized other is a legacy from our ancestors, partly old-fashioned, partly unfashioned; but it is gradually remade within the individuals working within it. The social world generalized in each self according to its experience is a reflection of what that world has been and a prognosis of what it may become.

VI

HOW THE NOVEL MINISTERS TO PERSONALITY

The reconstruction of society going on within the individual becomes apparent whenever a person expresses his view of life. The most popular medium of such expression at present is the novel. Through venting his own feelings the novelist voices what his group feels. That others live in common with him and welcome an expression of their life is his inspiration. While they are dumb he cries out when he feels the pinch, the rub between traditions, institutions, and human needs; he shows what the signs of promise are and holds up a vision of the things that may be hoped for. He shows where society is breaking down, and how it is being reconstructed.

If a realist he does this directly, if a romanticist he does it indirectly. The romantic response to social difficulty is to build up a self that lives in an extra-actual world; and the readiest way to get such a world is not to invent one outright, but to turn to the past, which may be imagined to contain what is wanting in the present. The Middle Ages, already idealized in old romance, needed only to be retouched by Sir Walter Scott to suit the taste of his own time. His characters hardly pretended to be historical, nor were they the heroes celebrated by the troubadours; they were contemporary

Englishmen in masquerade, their trappings medieval, their minds coeval. Given the period, the costumes, and castles, Scott had only to let his fancy play among them according to the ideal laws of the day-dream, write out his dreaming, and share it with his readers. What are the rules of the day-dream? If men are mean and women uninspiring, let there be chivalrous knights and beautiful, sighing ladies; if business is unadventurous and war is a bad business, let there be silken commerce with Cathay and Crusades against the Saracen; let there be circumstances which offer a delightful escape from our own.

Stevenson says:

> It is not character, but incident, that woos us out of our reserve. Something happens as we desire to have it happen to ourselves; some situation, that we have long dallied with in fancy, is realized in the story with enticing and appropriate details. Then we forget the characters; then we push the hero aside; then we plunge into the tale in our own person and bathe in fresh experience; and then, and then only, do we say we have been reading a romance. . . . . Fiction is to the grown man what play is to the child; it is there that he changes the atmosphere and tenor of his life; and when the game so chimes with his fancy that he can join in it with all his heart, when it pleases him with every turn, when he loves to recall it and dwells upon its recollection with entire delight, fiction is called romance.[1]

By this criterion the works of Dumas are the highest romance, for it is believed that no other writer has given so many people this sort of pleasure. A great French surgeon told Dumas' son: "All our hospital patients recover or die with one of your father's books under their

[1] "A Gossip on Romance."

pillow. When we wish to make them forget the terror of an approaching operation, the tediousness of convalescence, or the dread of death, we prescribe one of your father's novels, and they are able to forget."[2]

The push-off that romance takes from a troubled, painful world is confessed by George Sand in her foreword to *Mauprat*. She says she wrote it just after pleading for separation, when marriage, the abuses of which she had been combating, appeared to her in all the moral beauty of its principle. The more she thought how sad it was to break that bond the more she felt that what were lacking in marriage were the elements of happiness and equity of an order too exalted to preoccupy society as it actually is. So, she says, in writing a novel to occupy and distract herself, the thought came to her to paint an exclusive love, eternal, before, during, and after marriage. She says her feeling was summed up in these words of Mauprat near the end of the story: "She was the only woman that I loved in all my life; never did another attract my glance or know the pressure of my hand."

Compensation is also important in the work of Stevenson, struggling as he did against the most disheartening physical odds. In his thought he is classed as a modern stoic, but in his fiction he is thoroughly romantic. His scenes are laid in a colorful past and crowded with spirited adventure. Perhaps a critic never went further wrong than did William Archer in writing to Stevenson that his optimistic point of view was that of a hearty fox

[2] Quoted by James O'Donnell Bennett in an article on *The Three Musketeers* in the *Chicago Tribune*.

hunter, and that if he, Stevenson, ever had any ill health he would certainly modify it! When R. L. S. replied that he had been bed-ridden for nearly two years the critic expostulated that then he had no right to such an outlook! No heroes have more blood-red blood than his. Their characters are left conveniently blank so that the reader may easily insert his own self into the action. The first-person form of narrative so often used by him is an aid to this. Who is Jim Hawkins? Plainly, he is every boy who reads *Treasure Island*. And there is very little analysis of the other characters to distract the reader from the thrill of pure action. All that is necessary for the character of a pirate is a brace of pistols and gold earrings, with perhaps a wooden leg. A passage from one of Stevenson's letters shows what romance was to him.

> When I suffer in mind, stories are my refuge; I take them like opium; and I consider one who writes them as a sort of doctor of the mind. And frankly, ... it is not Shakespeare we take to, when we are in a hot corner; nor, certainly, George Eliot—no, nor even Balzac. It is Charles Reade, or old Dumas, or the *Arabian Nights,* or the best of Walter Scott; it is stories we want, not the high poetic function which represents the world; we are then like the Asiatic with his *improvisatore* or the middle-agee with his *trouvère*. We want incident, interest, action: to the devil with your philosophy. When we are well again, and have an easy mind, we shall peruse your important work; but what we want now is a drug. So I, when I am ready to go beside myself, stick my head into a story-book, as the ostrich with her bush; let fate and fortune meantime belabour my posteriors at will.[3]

In contrast with these romantic escape books, are the novels dealing with the world about us. When a

[3] *Letters* (Scribner's 1917 edition), I, 322.

novelist undertakes to treat things as they are, however, he finds, aside from the natural difficulties of the attempt, that romance has distorted vision and spoiled the perspective of homely things. Among the first duties of the realist, then, is the correction of romance. One of the greatest novels was written with that purpose, *Don Quixote,* which shows how too much reading about knight-errantry takes away common sense. Yet it also does justice to the beauty of the ideals of chivalry, and the poor old crazy nobleman can never become a comic character because the ideals which he exaggerates have been so wrought into the race that even absurd devotion to them stirs admiration. Our notions of courage and fidelity and honor, without which we are hardly better than the squire of Don Quixote, got into our social inheritance largely through *The Amadis of Gaul* and other books of chivalry in the library of Don Quixote, all of which are summed up in himself. The moral which Cervantes presents is not to give up these ideals, but to observe their spirit rather than their letter, for after all their letter never existed outside letters. The trouble is that people rarely have the imagination to take over the ideals of romance and adapt them; they would fain adopt them just as they are in books, failing which they sigh and dream away their time, only children having the quixotic courage to tinker a basin into a helmet and wear it in spite of ridicule. In his masterpiece Cervantes shows the intrinsic value of romantic ideals much as Plato in the second book of *The Republic* shows the true worth of justice by taking the case of a just man who is outwardly the most unfortunate of men, and as the author of the Book of Job shows that righteousness is disinterested love of God, and its own reward. Don Quixote in the greatest disgrace remains the master of the man who repeats the proverbs of the people. It is due to wicked enchantments that the old knight looks foolish to others; in itself his chivalry is a perfect thing.

The danger of romance is also shown in Flaubert's *Madame Bovary,* where it undermines Emma's mind. "She would like to have lived in some old manor, like those long-corsaged medieval ladies who passed their days beneath the trefoil of ogive windows, their elbows on the stone sill, chin resting on one hand, watching deep in the distance the approach of a cavalier with a white plume who gallops on a black horse."[4] She is unable to endure the prosaic country doctor who is her husband; her affairs with other men lose interest; she is ruined by her extravagance and driven to suicide. Yet she dresses and acts her part of a romantic lady in provincial Yonville with something of the feeling Don Quixote has for the male counterpart. The brains of both become addled,[5] but there is a difference. Romance inspires Don Quixote to be generous and gentlemanly, to go abroad to the relief of the weak and oppressed. The female version of the chivalric ideal, on the contrary, does not inspire thought of others and action in their

[4] *Madame Bovary,* 1re partie, chap. vi.

[5] "Madame Bovary n'avait pas encore l'intelligence assez nette pour s'appliquer sérieusement à n'importe quoi" (2me partie, chap. xiv). "Este sobredicho hidalgo . . . . se daba á leer libros de caballerías con tanta afición y gusto, que olvidó casi de todo punto el ejercicio de la caza, y aun la administración de su hacienda" (*Don Quijote,* Parte primera, cap. I).

behalf; it tells the fair reader to adorn herself and fold her scented hands, to withdraw within her tower whence she shall not even look upon the outside world except as she may see it dreamily reflected in her mirror.

A man may still get helpful stimulus from the ideal of chivalry. He may think of difficulties as giants challenging his prowess, as Don Quixote personified the windmills. But there is nothing analogous in the ideal of a knight's lady, with her swooning and her smelling salts, for the modern woman. Even for men romance is dangerous in tending to usurp the place of action, so that when the opportunity does come to be the hero one has dreamed of being, one may be unable to move, like Conrad's Lord Jim. Yet the fact that Lord Jim finally realized his dream in a plausible manner indicates that for clearness the term "romance" should be reserved for day-dreams which cannot be literally realized, which no sane person would seriously think of carrying out. Romance is a game, a relaxation. It is not an effort to live more fully, but to achieve a release from living. It is a flight from the actual to the impossible. "Adventure," on the other hand, plunges one deeper into actual life; it connotes an earnest striving for all that seems to be denied in tediously staying at home—life on the high seas and in far lands amid strange dangers. Adventure falls within the realm of the possible; it is not hopeless of actual attainment, like romance. No Yankee really hopes to reach King Arthur's court, but many Yankee boys have run away to sea, and this makes Jack London more thrilling to them than Mallory or Howard Pyle. The fascinating places he writes about are in the school atlas, and he was actually there himself. Whereas romance is other-worldly, adventure is on the other side of this world. A boy in Jack London's *Valley of the Moon* says:

> Don't you sometimes feel you'd die if you didn't know what's beyond them hills an' what's beyond the other hills behind them hills? An' the Golden Gate! There's the Pacific Ocean beyond, and China, an' Japan, an' India, an' . . . . an' all the coral islands. You can go anywhere out through the Golden Gate—to Australia, to Africa, to the seal islands, to the North Pole, to Cape Horn. Why, all them places are just waitin' for me to come an' see 'em. I've lived in Oakland all my life, but I'm not going to live in Oakland the rest of my life, not by a long shot. I'm goin' to get away . . . . away. . . . .[6]

The land as well as the sea excites the wanderlust. *The Travels of Marco Polo*, Parkman's *Oregon Trail*, Kipling's *Kim*, Hudson's *Green Mansions*—these and other tales of roaming give the reader the same value that he gets from sea stories. Adventure is seeing the world and making a man of one's self therein. More than the sight of exotic places, what is sought in adventure is a new self. Rebecca West calls it "forcing life's hand and leaping straight from boyhood to manhood by leaving school and becoming a sailor at sixteen."[7]

Romance is make-believe; adventure is believing one can make more of one's self somewhere else, almost anywhere far enough from home. But both are palliative

[6] *The Valley of the Moon*, pp. 263, 264.

[7] *The Judge*, p. 363. The spirit of adventure is beautifully expressed in Eichendorff's *Aus dem Leben eines Taugenichts:* "'Nun, sagte ich, wenn ich ein Taugenichts bin, so ist's gut, so will ich in die Welt gehen und mein Glück machen.'"

as regards the real problem of life. They do not directly aid people who have to stay at home in the real world, as all real people have to do after all, for wherever they go they carry their selves with them, as snails do their shells. Then, more valuable than tales of romance and adventure are novels which reveal the romance and adventure of reality, of every day, of staying at home. That is the revelation which people seek; and that they do find it in novels accounts for their interest in them. Most people realize when they reflect upon it that it matters little where they stay or whither they go, but that it makes all the difference in the world what kind of person they are. If one could only be the right kind of person everything would be all right. The key to all our difficulties is in personality, and it is because the novelists understand this that we read their books.

Man's chief preoccupation, after the maintenance of his animal being, is the development of his social self or personality. Since this self is developed through taking over the rôles of others, attention is constantly upon one's fellows. How to act in different situations, what are social errors, who are the best bred, and what is the excellence of their behavior—these are the questions which fill man's thought and conversation. But actual experience of society is never very wide: only a few individuals out of multitudinous mankind are present in any circle of acquaintance. The expansion of personality, however, need not be hampered by this circumstance. Let a man take a novel in his hand, it is to take up the compass of his character and draw a wider circle. What society may not be seen between the covers of a novel? Paris, London, Rome, our prairies, and the steppes of Siberia—everywhere is there, along with anthropology, psychology, history, and all the instruction that can be got without scientific application—no one ever picked up calculus from a novel!

The novel is most important, not as an avenue to romance or adventure, but as an approach to reality, which alone is ultimately interesting to a mature mind, which absorbs into itself every other interest. The novel is best understood as the final elaboration of play and day-dreaming. In play the personality is built up through taking over the rôles of others; and in play the personality which has been developed is expressed, or "given play," more freely than in the activities which happen to be assigned to one. The school tries to avail itself of the play-interest, but since it is essentially spontaneous and personal it can never be fully directed from without or supplanted, though it may well be guided and supplemented. Likewise a man's day-dreaming enters into his work, when he thinks about coming situations, perhaps lies awake at night rehearsing them, and pictures himself in the future. But it is rare that a man's interest is all absorbed in his overt occupation, and this is well, for it is due to his surplus curiosity about the world at large that he comes to know anything about it, to sympathize with it and adequately adjust himself to it. Through participating imaginatively in different rôles a man develops his personality just the same as the child does who impersonates different characters in his play; and like the child he is thereby enabled to air and exercise his various selves which are not allowed to appear in the house he lives in or the business he works at. Through play and the day-dream one escapes the accidents of birth, education, and occupation, and becomes a spirit free to take whatever form one likes and engage in whatever pursuit is alluring. Yet this need not be merely an escape, but rather another birth into the world, a new chance to explore it and come to know it, which cannot fail to make one more at home in one's own home as well as outside it. Play and day-dreaming permit one to bring home to one's self all the manifoldness of mankind, to share its endeavors and hopes and make them one's own, instead of remaining preoccupied with immediate interests which must seem petty in comparison. The movie and the newspaper and most forms of literature widen one's horizon, but the novel is the most direct continuation of play and day-dreaming. In the novel a man's repertory of rôles is augmented; his knowledge of human nature in all its manifestations is increased; and also his personality, which is only partially participant in his "real" relations, is given opportunity to exercise its most various capacities, meeting the people and the situations it craves, and freely expressing all its otherwise suppressed desires. It is no exaggeration to say that a reader of novels gets his character more from them than from his relatively restricted overt experience; and it is equally certain that more may be judged of his personality by the novels he reads than by the few visible deeds his outward lot permits him to perform. People are what they read; by their books shall ye know them.

It is not only remote countries and customs which

are brought home to one through the novel; the significance of one's own hearth is lighted up thereby. One tends to overlook what is familiar and close at hand, except as it falls within the aesthetic phase of response to a problem. One never really sees anything except as one sees it aesthetically. The immense importance of the novel lies just here: that everything within its covers is regarded aesthetically, contemplated leisurely and for itself, taken in without reserve, and perhaps for the first time really regarded with attention. The things about one which are ordinarily overlooked or taken for granted become aesthetic objects. The life about one which for the most part flows by unheeded becomes dramatic; life in itself is seen objectively and charged with meaning. All the blinding, narrowing force of a person's ordinary preoccupations and prejudices is in abeyance; he is off his guard, in a mood to absorb what would otherwise be shut out, and as a result comes to sympathize with persons and interests to which he would otherwise have remained hostile or indifferent; his personality is opened up and a whole section of the world is introduced every time he reads an important novel.

VII

THE RELATION OF FICTION TO REFLECTION

However remote they may seem from our lives, if novels do interest us it must be because they help us to live, by giving us cues and suggestions which we need. They could be interesting on what other basis? Novels differ in appeal to people because their needs are different; but the majority have problems in common to a degree insuring a certain unity of response to novels bearing upon fundamental matters.

Every type of social problem has novels dealing with it. Thus *Romola, The Cloister and the Hearth,* and *The Real America in Romance* by Edwin Markham, are novels recommended by historians for their historical value. But even inaccurate historical novels give a feeling for periods and persons that could not be rendered in any other way. Sober history itself grows largely out of sympathetic imagination and literary psychology. The usual trouble with historical novels is that they are romantic, that they are escapes from the present rather than sincere attempts to understand the past. Still, if people vicariously acquire some history through reading romance it should not be begrudged them. They may pick up *Le Chevalier de Maison Rouge* for diversion, and they will be gloriously diverted, but they will also smell the blood of the French Revolution.

Then there are novels dealing with religion. Such is Walter Pater's *Marius the Epicurean,* especially in the later chapters about the church in Cecelia's house where Marius discovers the joy and hope which Christianity has brought to the jaded Romans. The novels of Chateaubriand express the romantic fascination of the Catholic cult. *La Cathédrale,* by Huysmans, glories in its mysteries and symbolism. The conflict between religion and science is a common theme in recent fiction. *Doña Perfecta,* by Galdós, shows how the devout of a backward community in Spain are shocked by the unleavened materialism of a young engineer who has become contemptuous of religion. *La Catedral,* by Ibáñez, shows that loss of the old religious faith need not result in nihilism, for the hero feels that "he has to believe in something, to dedicate to the defense of an ideal the faith of his character." Social idealism takes hold of him and he determines to work for the evolution of humanity "like the first apostles of Christianity, sure of the future, but not in a hurry to see his ideas realized." The "faith of his character" which sustains him is very like the Undying Fire which burns in Wells's modern Job when all has gone against him and his faith in everything else is shaken. "And now that my heavens are darkened, now that my eyes have been opened to the wretchedness, futility, and horror in the texture of life, I still cling, I cling more than ever, to the spirit of righteousness within me." May Sinclair's *Mary Olivier,* after breaking from religion through reading philosophy, comes to find reality within herself in a kind of mystical insight. *The Way of All Flesh,* by Samuel Butler, after dragging a father and son through religious doubts, comes to the conclusion that the spirit of the church is all right, but its forms out of date. Hugh Walpole, in *The Cathedral,* represents the forms of religion and the cathedral itself as becoming the object of almost idolatrous worship. May Sinclair's *Cure of Souls* tells the story of a woman who thinks she is in love with God when she is only in love with the rector, who does not disabuse her mind because her illusion is of great convenience to his laziness, inasmuch as it leads her to do his hard work for him. The list might be lengthened, but it seems unnecessary to argue that the real interest which people have in religion and their perplexity about it constitutes the appeal of these novels.

There are few novels dealing explicitly with technical philosophy, but every novel presents a view of life and comes to some terms with the problems of philosophy. Walter Pater's *Marius* and May Sinclair's *Mary Olivier* are shown in reaction to different systems of thought. Herman Melville's *Moby Dick* is saturated with Emersonian transcendentalism. H. G. Wells writes constantly in the spirit of the pragmatic philosophy of James and Dewey, and every novelist who amounts to anything has a philosophy of some sort or other, and it is not amiss to speak of a great novelist as a philosopher. Professional philosophers are usually too engrossed in their ideas to dress them out in the form of fiction, though many of them have found this their best medium of expression, for it would not be wrong to consider as philosophical novels such works as Plato's *Republic,* More's *Utopia,* Campanella's *City of the Sun,* Bacon's *New At-*

lantis, Voltaire's *Candide,* Nietzsche's *Zarathustra.* A novel by a man who is really both a poet and a philosopher is a rare delight, and Santayana's admirers eagerly await the one he is writing. When Tolstoy turned to philosophy he looked back on his novels as part of his youthful folly, though he had actually put his best philosophy into them. But Dostoievsky deliberately put his philosophy into his fiction, though it is hard to see with Middleton Murry that *Crime and Punishment* is from beginning to end a commentary upon the system of Kant.

The novel is also concerned with most of the problems of physical and social science, the economic system, government, law, education, and especially love and marriage. It is pertinent first to take up the relation between art and thought, between fiction and reflection. Both arise within the problematic situation. Mr. Dewey says: "Any imagination is a sign that impulse is impeded and is groping for utterance. Sometimes the outcome is a refreshed and useful habit; sometimes it is an articulation in creative art; and sometimes it is a futile romancing which for some natures does what self-pity does for others. The amount of potential energy of reconstruction that is dissipated in unexpressed fantasy supplies us with a fair measure of the extent to which the current organization of occupation balks and twists impulse, and, by the same sign, with a measure of the function of art which is not yet utilized."[1]

Thwarted impulse issues most easily in "unexpressed fantasy." If this "futile romancing" be articu-

[1] *Human Nature and Conduct,* p. 164.

lated, it assumes the dignity of art. When does it become thought? The aesthetic attitude is located where the flow of habitual activity has been checked by a problematic situation, in the lull before reflection sets in. When we go on to reflect, to form a hypothesis and attempt a solution, we go beyond the aesthetic stage to that of reflection. The relation of art to thought is expressed by Santayana thus: "Man's intellectual progress has a poetic phase, in which he imagines the world; and then a scientific phase, in which he sifts and tests what he has imagined."[2] Art presents the data in a problem for their own sake; thought goes on to test them for the sake of the solution. When art is critical, as in George Meredith, it approaches thought; when science is in the stage of gathering data and imagining a picture into which they will fit, it is still in the aesthetic phase. With every advance it makes science admits its earlier achievements to have been imaginative and artistic, but valuable for science on account of their collection and conservation of data. Thus, astrology accumulated and kept data which were later of great use to astronomy; alchemy did the same for chemistry; the imaginative maps of early travelers decorated with sea monsters and gold mountains, did the same for geography; and mysticism did the same for psychology.

"Out of the space between an impulse and a reaction there arises an idea or 'presentation.' A 'presentation' is, indeed, it would seem, ... only a delayed, intensified desire—a desire of which the active satisfaction is blocked, and which runs over into a 'presentation.'

[2] *Reason in Art*, p. 76.

An image conceived, 'presented,' what we call an *idea* is, as it were, an act prefigured."[3] That is to say that ideas appear within a problematic situation as foreshadows of its solution. They are the first response to the problem in which we simply look at it. While we are looking the elements in it which will enable us to deal with it begin to transpire. These are the cues for response to the situation; they are its values; and contemplation of them constitutes the aesthetic experience. Art is the artifice for objectifying these values to facilitate our attention to them. Art never solves a problem; it merely represents the values which any solution must take account of. When we go on to test the representations of art, to reduce its epicycles to simpler laws, we leave the aesthetic attitude for that of reflection.

The consequence of art is reflection. Art leads us to contemplate values in an unguarded mood during which we surrender to the situation, and the result is that we cannot help thinking about what we have seen. In the drama and in the novel we are led to sympathize with persons and situations which we might otherwise ignore, and thereafter it is harder to shut them out and refuse to think about them. Art need not tell us what to think, it is best when it does not, but it forces us to think by placing a problematic situation before us, and we must continue to think until we have come to some satisfactory solution.

The adjustment which art leads to may be one of surrender, as in Greek drama, wherein the nobility of the individual is measured by the pathos of his tragedy.

[3] Jane Harrison, *Ancient Art and Ritual*, p. 53.

Shakespeare also accepts an established order to which the individual must succumb. Satire refuses to accept, yet points neither to escape nor reconstruction: it is negative. But comedy is positive and progressive in its effect. Whereas tragedy shows the individual acquiescing in society, comedy shows him breaking its conventions, thereby giving the audience vicarious release therefrom, and freedom to reflect thereon. Comedy dramatizes freedom; it makes fun of the established order that the individual may criticize it without feeling that he is breaking an inviolable law and destroying himself. Comedy is not futilely bitter against everything in general, nor is its fun the trifling of farce. It envisages an ideal order by which it may show up the foibles of society as it is, with the moral purpose of correcting them through "thoughtful laughter." Thus George Meredith says of Aristophanes: "There is an idea in his comedies; it is the idea of good citizenship. . . . . This laughing bald-pate, as he calls himself, was a Titanic pamphleteer, using laughter for his political weapon."[4]

The freedom and revolt of comedy arise in opposition to the acceptance taught by tragedy, and the greater the tragedy the greater the contemporary comedy, for the more inflexible and sacred the social order is represented to be, the more is it in need of criticism and reflection. It is because comedy is reflective that in comedy art approaches thought. Meredith says: "Philosopher and comic poet are of a cousinship in the eye they cast on life." Any absurdity or excess is a mark for comedy. After the romance of chivalry had taught

[4] *An Essay on Comedy.*

an exaggerated code of honor, appeared the picaresque story. Fielding followed the epic with the mock epic. Racine went back to classic tragedy, but Molière, like Aristophanes, made fun of contemporary folly, including the folly of too serious acceptance of tragedians.

Meredith's theory of comedy is best illustrated by his own novels. He deals with typical characters exaggerated into ideas which are fitted together in a plot designed to bring out their meaning. The characters being his own ideas, when he stands at the curtain and talks about them, as he continually does, their action and his reflection are felt to be all of a piece; there is pleasure and instruction in both; the art is thoughtful and the thought is artistic; to laugh with Meredith is to think with him. His is not an art of escape from, or acceptance of, the social order, but an art of reflection, of reconstruction and progress.

Tragedy, however, may lead on to reflection as well as comedy—not so much the tragedy of the Greeks or of Shakespeare perhaps, but that of Ibsen, for example, which does not foster acceptance of things as they are, but shows the necessity of doing something. This kind of tragedy, though it has a completeness of its own, yet requires a sequel in life. The only sequel to the other kind of tragedy is passivity and resignation, its moral being that self-realization is achieved through acceptance. But this tragedy is that something needs to be done which could be done, the moral being that man should revolt and reform. It is kinetic; it has consequences. Andreyev's *Red Laugh* is perhaps the most terrible indictment of war ever written. One cannot read it without reflecting and refusing to accept war. While it is too terrible for ordinary laughter, its title indicates its kinship with comedy. In comedy we laugh at incongruity; in this tragedy no laughter is equal to the madness of the absurdity but the headless Red Laugh.

Art does not tell us just how the good in life is to be increased and the evil diminished; that is the work of science. Art shows what we need for a fuller life, that our thought may be directed toward it. Wells does not specify just how men can become like gods, but in showing how attractive this dream is and in assuring us that it is attainable he urges us toward it. Every novelist gives the view of life which he thinks good. If it seems too visionary we put it under the category of Escape. If it tolerates things as they are or holds that nothing can be done we call it Acceptance. But if it holds up an unattained state which we think attainable we may classify it as Progress or Reconstruction, and it is this last type of novel which most arouses thought. Escape shirks thought and Acceptance regards it as unnecessary or impotent. But an ideal within possible reach stimulates us to think how we may approach it, and to put us in this state of mind is perhaps the supreme social achievement of literature.

To recapitulate the relation of art to thought: the aesthetic response to a problem gives way to the reflective and scientific attitude. Still we enjoy falling back into the aesthetic attitude in matters toward which we have long learned to be scientific, though not in the ingenuous, naïve way of those who have not begun to reflect. To take up an old aesthetic outlook is an escape from present problems, not an advance—as in the effort of some to live in the attitude of the Middle Ages. The mythology of the Greeks cannot have the same value for us as it had for them. The mythus or world-view of biology or psychology, with which science has not quite caught up, is perhaps more genuinely satisfying to us. To some extent science spoils poetry, as Darwin said it did for him; but it cannot hurt the poetry which is abreast or ahead of the age, no matter when it was written. There may be people who now read psychoanalysis instead of love stories, but this does not drive novelists from the subject, for science has hardly begun to sift the mystery out of it; science has merely forced the novelist deeper into the subject, as in the case of D. H. Lawrence and some of his contemporaries, who take all they can find in psychoanalysis and then plunge beyond it. The constant and insistent problems of conduct have hardly been touched by science; they continue to be the special province of the novelist, who is doing all he can to stimulate the scientist to follow him. The result of becoming more intelligent usually is, however, to become aware of more mystery, and thus to enhance the aesthetic response, so that it is doubtful if the artist will ever be supplanted by the scientist. It is much more likely that in the future every scientist will be an artist, regarding his research and reflection as preparation for his art, like Leonardo.

Wherever a problem presses the artist responds and the scientist prepares to follow. The scientist himself uses artistic imagery in approaching a problem and in forming his hypotheses. Artist and scientist often dwell in the same man. The artistic attitude tends to pass into science by its own momentum, and back to art. The same questions which led to mythology lead on to science, and back to myth; the same queries put more critically chasten art into thought, and then humanize thought into art. The fairy tales which satisfied the child's mind ultimately suit the adult, when "rationalized" and re-written in a manner as fascinating and convincing to the grown-up as the tales were to the child. Thus Shaw says the account in Genesis and the modern theory of evolution are two versions of the same thing. The more we learn about a subject the less are we satisfied with the initial artistic treatment of it, and the more we go on with it the more we find the scientific treatment of it to become like art, both in its imaginative advance and in the growing sense of the inadequacy of its past achievement. Science is artistic in its nascency, and it continues to be so on its frontiers. A candid scientist will confess that no set of symbols or formulas is final or absolute; that one is employed rather than another for social convenience, because it is established, accept-ed, and current, all of which comes very close to saying that the scientist is swayed in his thought by considera-tions which after all are aesthetic. The aesthetic atti-tude is forced by the pressure of a problem into the reflective, and, by the same drive, on again to the aes-thetic.

Logically there is first a problem, then contempla-tion of the values involved (the aesthetic stage), and then an effort to solve it (the reflective stage), leading to further contemplation, and so on in an endless cycle, all of which is mystically mirrored within the aesthetic phase itself. How long it takes to reach the reflective stage depends upon the urgency of the problem and how satisfying the aesthetic response to it is. To persist in the reflective attitude a moment longer than is necessary is unnaturally arduous. Yet the capacity for it can be educated, and modern science is proof of it. In ordinary life, however, reflection is short-winded and soon lapses into reverie whether successful or not, unless the problem be very insistent. But in organized science men may test and sift all their lives a problem which perhaps reached the aesthetic phase ages before. And in art other men specialize in aesthetic appreciation to an equal degree, though the influences in our society at present are more favorable to the scientists, because the race as a whole, in dealing with the problem of life as a whole, seems to be passing from art to science, though art will eternally endure.

As art leads to science, so the fact that in the past there has been more art than science, along with our fresh realization of the fact, accounts somewhat for the present industry of science in trying to make up for lost time. Old problems, too long in the aesthetic stage, cry out for belated research. The uncritical, merely imaginative view of them is becoming too inadequate. Then, too, as science is catching up in physical problems its backwardness in social questions becomes more evident, and our emotional interest in them, our long aesthetic attitude toward them, is itself carrying us into the effort to understand them more fully, for the things we love most are ultimately those we will study most. And where love is great we need have no fear that science will diminish it, for science guided by love is one with art.

VIII

THE NOVEL AND EDUCATION

Because the aesthetic attitude toward a problem logically precedes and in a sense includes reflection upon it, the novelist's treatment of social questions is generally preferred to the scientist's. The kind of social problem to which the novel answers is not simply a conflict between the individual and society, nor a mere matter of adjustment of the one to the other, but a reconstruction of society through the individual. The fact that society is made over through the individual centers interest on him as the growing-point of society. The first response to the problem is the aesthetic one of simply looking at the individual in this light, watching the changes and turnings in his growth, not as a private affair, but as freighted with social significance. Contemplation of this development is facilitated by artistic representation. Only literary art can represent character unfolding, and that most adequately through the long, flexible form of the novel, which expresses in emotional terms what is thrust upon attention by the problem of the relation of individual to social growth. It does not try to solve the problem; it leaves that to the thought which is sure to follow the aesthetic response to a real problem. After art comes science, to analyze its values and put them into such a statement that they can be not only appreciated but understood and controlled.

The contemporary emphasis upon the individual in the novel and upon case study in social science is not adventitious, as a comparison of the two reveals.

For instance, the fresh discovery of childhood by the novelist is met by the effort of the educator to understand afresh the nature of the individual child. Formerly the child was forced to learn through fear of punishment, or was incited by the hope of honor. The latter method proved more successful, but had the great social disadvantage that it stimulated the competitive spirit and bred the careerist. The result of it was that learning was not the means to a social end; it was not even valuable in itself, but was a way to get ahead of the other fellow. Thus the more intelligent a student was, the more selfish he was likely to become, until, like Julien Sorel in *Le Rouge et le Noir,* his ruling idea would be *il faut briller.* Julien slept with a picture of Napoleon; he chose to be a theological student instead of a soldier simply because at the moment this promised the better career. But since Stendhal the novelist has discovered how much spontaneous interest the child has in learning, and the educator is trying now to work with that interest chiefly in mind, broadening and directing the child's own curiosity instead of ignoring it by appealing solely to his competitive spirit.

It is interesting to compare the aesthetic attitude toward childhood and the problem of education in the first part of *Jean-Christophe,* by Romain Rolland, with the reflective attitude toward it in the second chapter of *The School and Society,* by John Dewey. M. Rolland begins by showing how the child eagerly extends his world from the crib to the room, to the house, and to the outdoors. "How many things there are in this room! He does not know them all. Every day he sets out on a voyage of exploration in this universe which is his."[1] Mr. Dewey says: "The child is already intensely active, and the question of education is the question of taking hold of his activities, of giving them direction." He says further that the child is first interested only in subjects that come directly home to him, that his education consists in enlarging the circle of these subjects, which the child is naturally eager to talk about. The novelist shows how the child's interest is often ignored. Little Jean-Christophe was sitting in a cart, crushed between the legs of his grandfather and the driver, and was perfectly happy. "He talked aloud, without troubling about any answer to what he said." (Mr. Dewey says the child's questions are not so much questions as comments upon what catches his attention.) "He watched the horse's ears moving. What strange creatures those ears were! They moved in every direction—to right and left; they hitched forward, and fell to one side, and turned backwards in such a ridiculous way that he burst out laughing. He would pinch his grandfather to make

[1] Goethe's Werther says in visiting the scene of his childhood: "Ich erinnerte mich so lebhaft, wenn ich manchmal stand und dem Wasser nachsah, mit wie wunderbaren Ahnungen ich es verfolgte, wie abenteuerlich ich mir die Gegenden vorstellte, wo es nun hinflösse, und wie ich da sobald Grenzen meiner Vorstellungskraft fand, und doch musste das weitergehen, immer weiter, bis ich mich ganz in dem Anschauen einer unsichtbaren Ferne verlor—Sieh, mein Lieber, so beschränkt und so glücklich waren die herrlichen Altväter! so kindlich ihr Gefühl, ihre Dichtung!" (p. 119).

him look at them; but his grandfather was not interested in them. He would repulse Jean-Christophe, and tell him to be quiet. Jean-Christophe would ponder. He thought that when people grow up they are not surprised by anything, and that when they are strong they know everything; and he would try to be grown up himself, and hide his curiosity, and appear to be indifferent."

It is not only ignoring the child's interest that makes him hide it. The speech on "The Flag of Their Country," in Kipling's *Stalky & Company,* shows how shocking it is to boys to have waved before them the things which are sacred to them. It is important to recognize with the novelist that the child does have interests which of themselves lead toward action. Says M. Rolland: "It is impossible to imagine what can be made of a simple piece of wood, a broken bough found alongside a hedge." And Mr. Dewey: "The child's impulse to do finds expression first in play, in movement, gesture, and make-believe, becomes more definite, and seeks outlet in shaping materials into tangible forms and permanent embodiment." M. Rolland: "In his head he had the map of all the ditches and hillocks of the region extending two kilometers round about the house, and when he made any change in the fixed ordering of the furrows, he thought himself no less important than an engineer with a gang of navvies; and when with his heel he crushed the dried top of a clod of earth, and filled up the valley at the foot of it, it seemed to him that his day had not been wasted." Mr. Dewey says: "Children simply happen to do things, and watch to see what will happen."

M. Rolland shows Jean-Christophe experimenting with a grasshopper. Mr. Dewey says: "But this can be taken advantage of, can be directed into ways where it gives results of value."

M. Rolland says: "Everything has its worth, man or fly. Everything lives—the cat, the fire, the table, the grains of dust which dance in a sunbeam." Mr. Dewey: "The imagination is the medium in which the child lives. To him there is everywhere and in everything that occupies his mind and activity at all, a surplusage of significance." M. Rolland: "He can even do without door-mat boats, and caverns in the tiled floor, with their fantastic fauna. His body is enough. . . . . He spends hours in looking at his nails and shouting with laughter. They have all different faces, and are like people that he knows. . . . . Or sometimes he used to lie on his back and watch the clouds go by; they looked like oxen, and giants, and hats, and old ladies, and immense landscapes."

Very important for the educator is the fact of the boy's spontaneous pleasure in the piano until his father begins to give him lessons, whereupon his magic box becomes an instrument of torture. "There is an end of the magic sounds, and fascinating monsters, and the universe of dreams felt in one moment. . . . . Nothing but scales and exercises—dry, monotonous, dull—duller than the conversation at meal-time, which was always about the dishes, and always the same dishes." Teachers now recognize that the trouble is in the lessons, that music, being a matter of sounds, should be first taught by ear instead of through reading notation, which to the child has nothing to do with music, and that practice should consist more of interesting pieces than of dull exercises, just as language is being taught more through interesting reading than through laborious grammar drill. This change is largely due to the better understanding of the child facilitated by the novelist, which shows that where education is separated from real interests it is artificial and ineffective.

In *My Antonía* Willa Cather stresses the difference between the children who have had "advantages" and those who have helped to break the sod, learning from life and poverty. Mr. Dewey says that there must somehow be preserved at school the attitude which the child formerly got at home when real work was done in the home. One way is to have the children learn carpentry at school, cooking, sewing, etc. Manual training gives the child a kind of work the progress of which he can readily appreciate; it avoids the passive classroom posture and leads the child to co-operate with others. The spontaneous curiosity and inquisitiveness characteristic of the child's mind cutside school should somehow be maintained inside. In *Le Livre de Mon Ami* Anatole France shows that books themselves are naturally fascinating to a boy at the bookstalls along the quays.[2] Mary Olivier's passion for books developed at home.

[2] "O vieux juifs de la rue du Cherche-Midi! naïfs bouquinistes des quais, mes maîtres, que je vous dois de reconnaissance. Autant et mieux que les professeurs de l'Université, vous avez fait mon éducation intellectuale ... C'est en furetant dans vos boîtes, c'est en contemplant vos poudreux étalages, chargés des pauvres reliques de nos pères et de leurs belles pensées, que je me pénétrai insensiblement de la plus saine philosophie."

"The library at Five Elms was very small. Emilius used it as a smoking-room; but it was lined with books," and here she read and read. When there was something she did not understand she asked the obliging "encyclopedia man."

Again and again it is shown how far the child's own interest will carry him. Jack London's autobiographical novels reveal how intense the desire to learn from books as well as from life may be on the part of a boy in the most difficult circumstances. He kept two library cards going and always had books under his shirt while he was selling newspapers, which protected him against the fists of other newsboys. *Martin Eden, John Barleycorn, The Mutiny of the Elsinore,* and finally Mrs. London's *Book of Jack London,* all tell the same story of a passion for life and letters which had little sympathetic school guidance, yet needed it, because the thirst for knowledge is not infallibly directed toward that which will quench it.

Rousseau showed his belief in the nature of the child, as well as in Mother Nature, in his *Émile*. Émile's teacher is nature, his education being more an effort to keep him from bad influences than to teach him anything. Nature, rather than authority, is to correct his mistakes. To the age of twelve he develops his senses and health; from twelve to fifteen he has his intellectual education, learning lessons from things, and acquiring a trade to guard against bad fortune; at sixteen God is shown him in nature, and conscience in man. In contrast to *Émile* is *Richard Feverel,* by George Meredith, written to show the folly of raising a boy on a system. Then there is *Clark's Field,* by Robert Herrick, showing the danger of an education without any system. In *Joan and Peter* H. G. Wells points out that teaching can never be satisfactory until there is a pedagogic science. He says:

> It became manifest . . . . that the real work of higher education, the discussion of God, of the state and sex, of all the great issues in life, while it was being elaborately evaded in the formal education of the country, was to a certain extent being done, thinly, unsatisfactorily, pervertedly even, by the talk of boys and girls among themselves, by the casual suggestions of tutors, friends, and chance acquaintances, and more particularly by a number of irresponsible journalists and literary men. . . . . If the schools showed nothing to their children of the Empire but a few tiresome maps, Kipling's stories, for all his Jingo violence, did at least breathe something of its living spirit.[3]

Wells, more than most novelists, ventures to take the reflective as well as the artistic attitude toward a problem. He *shows* that the schools have failed to meet the needs of real children growing up in a real world, and he *says* that it is legitimate for their education to be supplemented by literary men, for while these men often "season wholesome suggestions with a flavour of scandalous excitement," they do write freely, they deal with the important issues, and in the end do more good than harm in that they do cause young people to think.

The novelist is vividly aware of the spontaneous interest in the child; he shows that his activities and remarks should be taken, not simply as amusing or annoying to his elders, but as having intrinsic importance, as worthy of attention and guidance. The wise educator agrees with the novelist. For instance, it is found that

[3] *Joan and Peter,* pp. 271–73.

the imagination of children around seven years of age recurs to the activities of primitive peoples. This is brought out in the chapter on the "Awakening of Jon Forsyte," in Galsworthy's *Forsyte Saga:*

> On this pond, after his father and Garratt had ascertained by sounding that it had a reliable bottom and was nowhere more than two feet deep, he was allowed a little collapsible canoe, in which he spent hours and hours paddling, and lying down out of sight of Indian Joe and other enemies. On the shore of the pond, too, he built himself a wigwam about four feet square, of old biscuit tins, roofed in by boughs. In this he would make little fires, and cook the birds he had not shot with his gun, hunting in the coppice and fields, or the fish he did not catch in the pond because there were none.

It is possible, says Mr. Dewey, "to utilize this interest so that it shall become a means of seeing the progress of the human race." It is not hard to get children to imagine civilized conditions removed and to picture those of hunting life. Thence they may be led in imagination through the stages of semi-agriculture and agriculture. The child's idea of primitive weapons leads naturally to a lesson in mineralogy through an examination of stones to find which are suited to various purposes. Always, continues Mr. Dewey, instruction is properly not given ready-made, cut and dried; it should be sought by the children in the course of their own curiosity and then worked out with them experimentally. Discussion of the iron age may lead to building a clay smelting oven and "instruction in principles of combustion, the nature of drafts and of fuel." Then the physical conditions implied in different forms of social life lead to a lesson in geography. Always the interest must be there before the information is given. This is not only more instructive than a system of set lessons, but it gives more training to the faculties of attention and interpretation. Novelists have shown that it is the way children do learn outside school where they have a chance, and it is now being taken over by the school itself, and rationalized.

This is to adapt education to the best interest of the child, rather than to warp the child to an unsympathetic system, as was done in the education of Arnold Bennett's Edwin Clayhanger.

> [He knew] nothing of natural history, and in particular of himself, ... not one word of information about either physiology or psychology. . . . . Geography had been one of his strong points. He was aware of the rivers of Asia in their order . . . . but he had never been instructed five minutes in the geography of his native county. . . . . For him history hung unsupported and unsupporting in the air. In the course of his school career he had several times approached the nineteenth century, but it seemed to him that for administrative reasons he was always being dragged back again to the middle ages. . . . . For his personal enjoyment of the earth and air and sun and stars, and of society and solitude, no preparation had been made or dreamt of.

His father's only regret was that another boy had beaten him in the examination. "'Well, that's a pretty how d'ye do! . . . . Going down one! Ye ought to ha' been first instead o' third. And would ha' been, happen, if ye'd pegged at it.' . . . . His father had enjoyed success with dogs through treating them as individuals. But it had not happened to him, nor to anybody in authority, to treat Edwin as an individual."[4]

The spirit of democracy requires recognition of the

[4] *Clayhanger,* chap. ii.

individual as such, whether child, woman, worker, citizen, or criminal. In marriage the woman as well as the man must be treated as a person rather than be defined in terms of an inherited institution. In economic life the worker must share in the social significance of his labor instead of being treated as part of the machinery. The criminal must be regarded by the law as an individual to be understood and cured if possible—one possessed of common human nature after all. The government likewise must not be imposed from without, but must come to represent individual freedom and responsibility. And in all these fields the twin attitudes of the aesthetic and the reflective response to the problem of the reconstruction of society through reformation of the individual are represented by the portrayal of personality in the novel and by the case study in social science.

IX

THE NOVEL AND LOVE AND MARRIAGE

The novelist has represented the individuality of the woman as well as that of the child, with the same spirit of discovering something too long ignored. The child was not to be taken seriously until through education he had ceased to be a child—and his education was defective for this very reason, that he was not considered as a person. Woman, however, was not only denied personality to begin with, but was forbidden the opportunity of developing it through education. She was allowed to have feelings, but not the discretion of their proper government—that would have been too high a prerogative for her. Thus Clarissa Harlowe complains in many a letter that her father and family regard her as a disobedient and unnatural girl because she refuses to place her tenderest emotions entirely at their disposal.

Another consequence of denying personality to woman was that lifelong companionship with her had to be contracted solely upon an emotional and instinctive basis. The flimsiness of this basis has been exposed in many novels of sentiment. They show that it is a pure accident if a girl kept strictly within her family, like Clarissa, should bestow her affection upon a worthy person. She has so little chance for choice and judgment that it were almost better for her to forego their exercise. The man, on his side, can be no more rational than his partner in such a mutual relation. When young ladies are secluded he too is reduced to the dilemma of marriage by family arrangement or love at first sight. The Abbé Prévost has shown that if he be a susceptible youth like the Chevalier des Grieux and meet an irresistible but frivolous and faithless young lady like Manon, the outcome is nearly mathematical,[1] though not unemotional. Paul de Saint-Victor says of *Manon Lescaut:* "Ce petit livre a la fièvre; il brûle, il palpite."

Since men and women do have characters, frivolous, noble, or otherwise, and since it is the whole personality which must be lived with in a full cohabitation, it ought

[1] The Avis de l'Auteur shows the Abbé's conception of the relation between the aesthetic attitude toward ethics presented in the novel and our reflection upon the subject. "Outre le plaisir d'une lecture agréable, on y trouvera peu d'événements qui ne puissent servir à l'instruction des moeurs; et c'est rendre, à mon avis, un service considérable au public que de l'instruire en l'amusant.

"On ne peut réfléchir sur les préceptes de la morale sans être étonné de les voir tout à la fois estimés et négligés, et l'on se demande la raison de cette bizarrerie du coeur humain, qui lui fait goûter les idées de bien et de perfection dont il s'éloigne dans la pratique. Si les personnes d'un certain ordre d'esprit et de politesse veulent examiner quelle est la matière la plus commune de leurs conversations, ou même de leurs rêveries solitaires, il leur sera aisé de remarquer qu'elles tournent presque toujours sur quelques considérations morales. Les plus doux moments de leur vie sont ceux qu'ils passent, ou seuls ou avec un ami, à s'entretenir à coeur ouvert des charmes de la vertu, des douceurs de l'amitié, des moyens d'arriver au bonheur, des faiblesses de la nature qui nous en éloignent, et des remèdes qui peuvent les guérir. Horace et Boileau marquent cet entretien comme un des plus beaux traits dont ils composent l'image d'une vie heureuse. Comment arrive-t-il donc qu'on tombe si facilement de ces hautes spéculations, et qu'on se retrouve sitôt au niveau du commun des hommes? Je suis trompé, si la raison que je vais en apporter n'explique bien cette contradiction de nos idées et de notre conduite: c'est que, tous les préceptes de la morale n'étant

to be fully considered before entering upon union. But in this story neither of the lovers is able to consider anything. Manon is seductive, frivolous, and faithless; he is susceptible, and the course of their love is inevitable. She cannot do without money, no matter what she has to do to get it; and he cannot do without her, no matter what he has to put up with.[2]

In *La Dame aux Camélias,* Alexandre Dumas *fils* discloses that even a *fille de joie* may have a soul, though he feels that this is an exception. But Marguerite's depiction of the attitude toward her class gains significance with the realization that it has been more or less the common attitude toward all women. "We have naturally no friends. We have egoistic lovers who

---

que des principes vagues et généraux, il est très difficile d'en faire une application particulière au détail des moeurs et des actions.

"... Dans cette incertitude, il n'y a que l'expérience ou l'exemple qui puisse déterminer raisonnablement le penchant du coeur. Or l'expérience n'est point un avantage qu'il soit libre à tout le monde de se donner; elle dépend des situations différentes où l'on se trouve placé par la fortune. Il ne reste donc que l'exemple qui puisse servir de règle à quantité de personnes dans l'exercice du vertu.

"C'est précisement pour cette sorte de lecteurs que des ouvrages tels que celui-ci peuvent être d'une extrème utilité, du moins lorsqu'ils sont écrits par une personne d'honneur et de bon sens. Chaque fait qu'on y rapporte est un degré de lumière, une instruction qui supplée a l'expérience; chaque aventure est un modèle d'après lequel on peut se former; il n'y manque que d'être ajusté aux circonstances où l'on se trouve. L'ouvrage entier est un traité de morale réduit agréablement en exercice."

[2] "Il n'estime plus Manon, il la méprise même, mais il lui est plus facile de devenir malhonnête que de passer d'elle ... Les caresses de sa chère maîtresse engourdissent son âme et sa conscience jusqu'à y étouffer la voix du remords" (quoted from Gauthier-Ferrières, in the Larousse edition of *Manon Lescaut,* p. 15).

spend their fortune, not for us, as they say, but for their own vanity. . . . . We are no longer beings, but things. We are the first in their self-love, and the last in their esteem."[3] Marguerite often read *Manon Lescaut,* "and she always told me that when a woman loves she cannot do what Manon did." Her tragedy is that she had already done it when she met Armand. "When God permits love to a courtesan, that love, which at first seems a pardon, becomes almost always a punishment to her." Marguerite's final proof of her love is to sacrifice it for the sake of her lover.

It was because Armand loved her for herself that she loved him: "parce que me voyant cracher le sang tu m'as pris la main, parce que tu as pleuré, parce que tu es la seule créature humaine qui ait bien voulu me plaindre." Men are so powerfully attracted by woman as woman that they often fail to know her as a person: then they do not know her, they know only what she looks like.[4] Thus it is better to become well acquainted before falling in love, than to fall in love first and then get acquainted. Another thing which often hinders a man's loving a woman for herself is the romantic tendency to love instead his own idea of her, and this is well portrayed by Marcel Proust. Albertine first appeared to him on the beach at Balbec, her companions beside her, the blue sea behind her, statuesque, classic, like a nymph on a shore of Greece.[5] For a long time his imagination worked over that scene before he met her. When he

[3] *La Dame aux Camélias,* chap. xv.

[4] As Emma says in *The Poor Man,* by Stella Benson.

[5] *A l'Ombre des Jeunes Filles en Fleurs.*

did come to know her he got different impressions of her every day, but underneath them all a continuity like a subterranean passage always led him back to the first Albertine, against the background of the sea. Proust pities those who are too impatient to wait through a period of imaginative anticipation, who jump into a carriage and drive directly to the object of desire. He observes that the most beautiful women in his life were those whom he glimpsed only and then lost sight of around a corner. He would drop everything to follow such a one through the crowd, but if so unlucky as to see her closely, or to get to know her, he discovered that she had faults. It was not her beauty after all which had struck him like a *coup de foudre,* but the momentary illusion that it was hers; it was really his idea of beauty which he unconsciously embodied in her so long as he did not see her closely enough to realize the discrepancy. But, says Proust, if one does not force love too fast one may gradually weave a dream about another person so firmly that it will gloss every fault with glamor.

The imagination, however, may bring about disillusion instead of warding it off. A poetic youth too readily idealizes any maiden who attracts him, endowing her with the graces of nymphs and goddesses, until she discovers to her sorrow that it is his own ideal which he worships. "Ne me regarde pas, je suis laide," said one of Jean-Christophe's first loves. In reading *Ariel* one may wonder why Shelley should have eloped with a little girl who had nothing to recommend her to anyone else but her blond hair and her blue eyes. But while others saw her as they imagined her to be, Shelley saw her as *he* imagined her to be, and his imagination surpassed theirs. The trouble was that it turned in other directions. Yet it may be said that when his ideal became objectified in another form he was not fickle to leave the first; he was following the gleam; he was faithful to his ideal wherever it appeared. He was a disciple of Plato, whose idealism arose from his own amorous experiences, as may be gathered from the *Symposium,* which teaches that at first one is drawn to the beauty of one form, then to that of another, until one learns that the various lovely forms of earth are merely manifestations of that heavenly beauty which alone is worthy of love, and which should be loved alike in whatever form it happens to appear. The poet, then, instead of being the most fickle of men, is the most steadfast. He seeks beauty everywhere until he realizes that the shapes thereof to be found on earth are all but shadows of the ideal which dwells in heaven. To that his soul finally flies. Nothing short of that will satisfy him. He is like other lovers in that he cannot be content with favors from the beloved; he cannot rest with anything that comes from her; he wants only her. But to him all earthly loves are only tokens from the celestial. He cannot be happy with any of them. "I do not want that which issues from you, but only want you, O sweet Love!"[6]

It is the poet's disillusion, then, in the wake of his impulsive effort to embody the infinite in the finite,

[6] "Non voglio quello che esce da te, ma sol voglio te, O dolce Amore!"—SANTA CATERINA DI GENOVA.

which ultimately saves him. What he had seemed to lose on earth he finds in heaven. But the poor child who loves the poet, she is no poet. She does not aspire to heaven, but to him whose love for a moment had lifted her to heaven. The poet after all is as selfish toward woman as the ordinary egoist. Where the latter requires her to be merely a submissive female, the poet thinks of her as his divine lady, an angel: neither is willing to accept her as a fellow human being and love her just for herself; to each she is a symbol of what he is seeking, a vessel of love, sacred or profane, and not the object of love itself. By each in his own way she is more adored than understood. And rather than take this worshiping what she represents, almost she would prefer a whipping for what she is. Almost she would rather be kicked for what she is than kissed for what she is not.

One lover is too fine, the other too coarse. Often the woman must face this dilemma of Mariflor in *La Esfinge Maragata,* by Concha Espina.[7] Rodrigo is a poet. He falls in love with Mariflor when the two share a sunrise from their compartment on the train, for at first sight she is all that his poetic imagination would make her; he is dazzled by the sun, and he leaves her before he can be disillusioned. With the enchantment of distance lent to the first impression he proceeds to send her love letters in his tenderest manner, with inclosures of poetry. All his idealism, all his exaltation in the presence of the stars and the sea, not omitting the sunrise they had shared, he focuses upon a sensitive, lonely girl from the city, exiled in a backward rural community

[7] Translated into English with the title of *Mariflor.*

with her grandmother. Her life being more dull than that of most girls, the letters from Rodrigo occupy all her thoughts and hopes. Finally, when he comes to see her, he realizes what he has realized countless times before: that she has been just a passing focus for the rays of his imagination, which are already shifting, refusing to be fixed, in spite of the pangs from his sense of honor and his sincere sympathy for Mariflor. So he passes from her life. Meanwhile the extreme poverty of her grandmother's household has made it seem her duty to marry Antonio, a rich peasant whose very presence offends her, because only on that condition will he give her family the help they must have. The priest persuades her to accept Antonio and find her consolation in religion, where she would have been forced to find it even if she had married the other.

In *Anna Karenina* Tolstoy has contrasted the wholesome happiness of Levin and Kitty in their married life with the disillusion attending the effort of Anna and Wronsky to enjoy a romantic and illicit love. The evil of trying selfishly to get thrills out of love without really meeting the conditions of love is also well illustrated in *Le Rouge et le Noir,* by Stendhal. Never, says the author, were such passionate words exchanged so coolly as between Julien and Mathilde. Both wanted to gain love without loving, and the emptiness in each heart was echoed in the hollowness of the other. In desperation they became more and more subtle in their amorous advances and retreats, entangling themselves in a web they could never unravel. Distrustful and deceitful, their reconciliations became more rare and difficult until it was impossible for them to share an honest emotion.

Novelists show more and more that love is not worthy of the name when regarded as an amusement or a game in which it is fair to cheat. They show that it really comes into being as a serious personal relationship, and that hence it is impossible when the personality of either or both is not considered. When the personality of woman has been ignored, true love has been very difficult. If it has been more dishonorable for a man to cheat at cards than to be unfaithful to a woman this is because his honor has not been involved in relations with women, since they were not regarded as persons. And laxity in women has not been so much a dishonor to them as an affront to the egoism of men, for women were thought incapable of honor. Women have belonged to men who did not belong to them, as George Meredith brings out in *The Egoist* in a way most embarrassing to the male reader. The hero could not make up his mind which of his feminine admirers should be accorded the inestimable favor of his choice, and he resented their inconsiderateness in finally marrying someone else instead of waiting indefinitely for him to decide. Finally he became engaged to Clara Middleton, who was worthy of the most generous love. But his egoism prevented his understanding that love is a gift. He was a fine youth, "he was anything but obtuse," yet he could not see how he offended her. He did not realize that he made her feel like "purchaseable stuff that has nothing to say to the bargain." The same thing happened in *The Portrait of a Lady*, by Henry James, in which Isabel Archer was a "caged bird" in relation to Gilbert Osmond, an aesthete who cared only for the curves and surfaces of beautiful things, including his wife, which he liked to collect and arrange to exhibit his perfect taste, so that for her to have a personality which was anything more than a reflection of his own was only a source of vexation to him.

The corollary to the subjection of a woman to a man is the loss of her free friendship with other men, and of his with other women. This is the theme of *The Passionate Friends,* by Wells. "To all other women he must be a little blind, a little deaf, politely inattentive. He must respect the transparent, intangible, tacit purdah about them." The heroine says: "Is there no way out of this? . . . . Because if there is not, then I had rather go back to the hareem than live as I do now imprisoned in glass—with all of life in sight of me and none in reach." But women are not going back; they are coming out; and this creates what Wells calls in the same book "a new situation for which there is as yet no tradition of behavior . . . . that new human comedy that is just beginning in the world, that comedy in which men still dispute the possession and the manner of possession of women according to the ancient rules, while they on their side are determining ever more definitely that they will not be possessed."

Formerly independence on the part of a woman meant being an adventuress, like Becky Sharp; but now it means demanding consideration as a person rather than as a woman merely. That is the attraction of Sheila Kaye-Smith's Joanna Godden, of Galsworthy's

Fleur Forsyte, Dorothy Richardson's Miriam, and May Sinclair's Mary Olivier. To be a person does not necessarily mean to be mannish. If it has seemed so it is because hitherto only the masculine personality has been recognized, so that to be a person a woman had to assume the rôle of a man, as Joanna Godden did. Yet woman's temperament and occupation have always been more personal than man's. As Professor Tufts says (in Dewey and Tufts's *Ethics*), her work of the household resists system, whereas man's work is usually standardized. Her contacts are face to face and complete; she has to deal with the "whole child," the "whole house," whereas the man deals only with parts of life, to which his professional manner makes an impersonal adjustment. Still he persists in thinking his world more important than woman's, and himself more of a person for participating therein, while woman has been forced to avow it, since his world has been organized and recognized independently of her, while hers has been isolated and ignored unless *he* deigned to notice it. His work, says Mr. Tufts, "is a constant stimulus, as well as support. A woman's work in the family has no such professional stimulus or professional vindication." This is well illustrated by Walpole in *The Cathedral*. The archdeacon is a personage through his work, while his wife is a person at all only through being his wife. Mr. Tufts says further: "If she does not see the whole of the husband, it is quite likely that the part not brought home—the professional or business part of him—is the most alert, intelligent, interesting phase." This also is brought out in *The Cathedral*. The archdeacon's wife cannot understand the town's admiration for him, since he is far from admirable as she knows him, for he demonstrates no interest in her or her housekeeping other than to take his meals and sleep at home. Formerly, when he was as much interested in her as he now is in his work, she had been fully able to admire him. Were he to take some interest in their children they might continue to have something in common; but he disregards them along with everything else in the house except his comfort and his library. He misses the education in parental affection by forbidding the children to talk at table or in any way press their presence upon him. He is unaware of fault; he is not deliberately mean; his center of interest is outside the home. He is not more self-sufficient than his wife; if he can get along without her companionship it is because he finds company outside; but when she is forced to sustain her own soul from without he cannot understand.

Neither of them, however, can get elsewhere the peculiar quality of the association they lose at home. The family elicits traits of affection which do not occur outside it, so that when the children and parents lose touch there is an absolute loss all the way around. The difference in age in itself tends to sever them, especially if times are rapidly changing, so that the children live in a world quite different from that of their elders, as in Turgenev's *Fathers and Sons*. If the family be immigrant, like the one in Willa Cather's *My Antonía,* the children adapt themselves far more readily than their parents to the new conditions, and the family solidarity is disrupted. But the most pathetic break between parents and children is not that caused by participation in different worlds outside the family, but the misunderstanding that arises within, before the children have stirred abroad. Mary Olivier is afraid of her father before she is out of the cradle. He never tries to enter the children's circle sympathetically, but breaks in upon it from time to time to tease and annoy them. Such conduct comes from the man's not putting his personality into the home, not treating the members of it as persons, neither his wife nor her children. He would not dare act that way away from home, knowing he would suffer for it. But at home he is a monarch above the law, free to abuse others, to order them about, or relax himself in amusement at their expense. He may not be a bad fellow; he may simply not realize that his home ought to be a democratic circle of individual persons, and so he lays aside his own civil personality when he comes back to them. Thus, in Katherine Mansfield's story, *At the Bay,* we can sympathize with the relief of the women and children of the household after the man has left in the morning, when the erstwhile autocracy quickly reverts to a republic.

Not only does such a selfish attitude toward the family cut the man off from its socializing influence, but it also impoverishes the larger life of the family when the one who by his broader experience might be the most stimulating member of it is indifferent to it and places his interest beyond it, making a mystery of his business, like Darius Clayhanger, instead of sharing it with the others. Too often the one person who could directly inform the family of the wider world is incommunicative. While there are exceptions to this, the novelist gives the impression that they are few.

Isolation within the home has obscured the personality of both woman and child. But the industrial revolution which has taken man out of the home, more than ever war did in the past, is at last emancipating woman even when she stays at home. It is still difficult, however, for her to achieve the fullest development at home, even when she is free to do so, for leisure is not enough. Whether her husband keeps her in luxury or in drudgery, it is not conducive to woman's self-respect that he has to give her money, with the implication that he is more important, since he was paid that which she must accept as a gift from him. His work is both remunerated and respected apart from her, whereas hers is neither paid nor praised except by him. Nevertheless, if they be a generously loving couple this is immaterial; his appreciation is worth more to her than that of the world, and he will not deem her labor lost because it is done solely for love of him and their children. It is an economic accident that their salary check should be made out to him rather than to her, her work being just as valuable to society as his, and often more indispensable. If the husband relieves the wife of all duties except that of devotion to him, that is a different matter, and it is likely that instead of increasing his respect for her, he will then not even render her that due a servant, as Ibáñez has shown in *La Maja Desnuda*.

When the wife is kept as a mistress, her power over her husband is as temporary as that of a mistress, for man's amorous nature is volatile and woman's charm transitory. But the appeal of her personality may be permanent. This is increasingly true as woman becomes emancipated and educated, freer to carry on interests beyond the home and thereby to bring the intellectual aspects of civilization within the home. It is no longer necessary for a wife to be denied a full life and the personal attraction that goes with it. No longer should it be possible to treat her merely as a woman and not as a person. Bad as that has always been, it is worse now that woman is already conscious of her right to personality. She will refuse to stay in the house as a chattel, like Irene in the *Forsyte Saga.* Men like Soames Forsyte will have to realize that woman is not property; and they will be happier for the discovery, as Young Jolyon was.

Since family life is essentially social, those who enter into it selfishly must fail to find its meaning. It should be harder to make this mistake, however, in face of the growing conviction that woman should be a person with rights of her own. Psychic incompatibility should occur less frequently when marriage is based more upon common education and interest. It is usually because personality is not sufficiently considered in the beginning that disagreeable personal differences are discovered later. Only a union based upon harmony of permanent traits can promise lasting satisfaction.

Most novelists agree in a view of life in which sex plays only a part. Thus Mary Olivier, though lonely, is happy with philosophy and music and work. Yet while sex is put in its place by the novelists, it is not regarded as unclean, so that though Mary Olivier does not continue her *liaison,* neither does she regret it. Joanna Godden buries her heart in her work when her love is thwarted. She severely dismisses a servant-girl who she thinks should have been married, and is greatly upset when her married sister runs away from her husband with another man; but when she herself is with child without being married she thinks it is not so bad if only she can move away where she can live unmolested. *The Judge,* by Rebecca West, is a cry against the obsession of sex. It glories in the complicated brains men carry in their heads and in their long hours of interest in sexless things. Richard's highest praise for his sweetheart is that her mind has as neat ankles as her body.

The novel does not solve the problem of marriage, nor any other problem, but it presents the material to be used in a reconstruction of the legal and conventional attitude toward it. It represents the values in the relation of man and woman quite apart from the institution of the family. By this institution's standard the relation may be regarded as a sin. But the novelist, in bringing out its values for their own sake, makes possible a consideration of them on their own merit and facilitates a change in attitude toward them. For instance, in *The Dream,* Wells has shown how the family on its present basis often fails to recognize the values in sex; it often sunders those whom God hath joined together, and joins those whom he hath sundered. Great steps are being taken in revamping educational institutions. In the juvenile court all definitely fixed legal procedure is laid aside in the effort to see just what is involved in the individual case. A realization of this reconstruction which is taking place in the institutions of law, education, politics, and economics should give a background for a readjustment toward sex. Because we are so intimately interested in it, it is harder to regard it objectively. It is so veiled with taboos and superstitions that we lack the courage to face it sincerely. There is evidence that our attitude toward it is changing, but we go on assuming that the ancient institutional point of view in regard to it need not be modified. Meanwhile the novelist continues to represent the situation as he sees it, throwing no stones and no bouquets at the institutional attitude (when he understands his business), but supplying the materials to be used in a reconstruction thereof.

The novelist enables us to free ourselves from the prejudices of our everyday life and contemplate the human values in love just for themselves. Then we see that sometimes the institution fits and fosters them; again that it distorts and disturbs them. For a moment, by grace of the aesthetic attitude induced by the skill of the novelist, we are empowered to consider the spirit at the expense of the letter, and not vice versa, as we are ordinarily required to do by the practical exigencies of life. In these aesthetic moments when we are freed from the fetters of respectability and all that is demanded of us by convention we see things dispassionately and are thereby led to check up and criticize our habitual judgments. In the aesthetic attitude we are off our guard, we sympathetically consider situations and persons which ordinarily we avoid or ignore. Something of this insight remains with us, so that our former attitude is insensibly altered. We become wiser and more humane for every good novel which we allow to affect us; and it is through novels more than through limited actual intercourse that we come to understand what Charles Reade called "all sorts and conditions of men."

From many novels one gets the notion that the trouble with love is marriage: that either lovers cannot get married, or they are afraid to, or they do. But from others one is convinced that the trouble with marriage is love, or rather the lack of it; and they show that only in marriage does love find its highest manifestation, when that which begins as a selfish passion is transmuted into self-effacing loyalty to the common good of the family. Such novels as *Anna Karenina, The Growth of the Soil* by Knut Hamsun, *The Great Hunger* by Johan Bojer show how love is ennobled by planning and striving and enjoying and suffering together; show that then it becomes infinitely finer than the moonstruck, romantic notion of it. These sunlit novels indicate that the disillusion, fickleness, and frivolity so often attendant upon romance are due to shallowness of character or ignorance, that the love of those who understand never faileth, and that it alone is love. It is true that people tire of what they possess; but wise lovers never allow themselves to be entirely possessed; they maintain their individuality by living in separate houses if need be, but especially by their separate thoughts, so that they never become stale to each other, or inattentive. They realize that marriage is not easy, that it is not achieved by the magic of a ceremony, but is the most difficult of the arts, requiring the utmost intelligence and tact. They see that the many misunderstand, abuse, and spoil it, while the "emancipated few" mistake it for a low estate suitable only to mediocrity. They see that marriage is not an opportunity to let down and let go, but a challenge and an avenue to spiritual development. They also see that while marriage is the only relation between the sexes that will satisfy them, there are other relations which may be preferable for those incapable of marriage.

The novel is of transcendent importance at present, because by portraying the development of character it shows how the individual absorbs the society about him, reacts to it, and reshapes it. The novel publishes the "discovery" that despite the impersonal organization of society, it is constituted by individuals, and thereby facilitates facing the problem of reconstructing society through the individual. Whereas the individual has heretofore been defined too much in terms of the institution, the novel is leading the way to a new Copernican revolution which will see the individual as the center and mover of the social order. Society is made over through change in the individual. Its customs and conventions imposed on him from without are old and conservative; his reactions thereto are fresh and reconstructive. His self is social; he gets it from the group; but as a new nexus it introduces novelty throughout all the rays of its interdependence. Hence the novelist's representation of the life of the individual focuses upon the growing-point of society. A comparison of his work with that of the social scientist shows the relation of art to thought. The problem of social progress has thrust the individual into attention as its key. The novelist presents him in his pivotal position as an object for aesthetic contemplation, making no attempt to turn the key, to offer a solution; while the scientist begins with the key which the novelist has found and tries to turn it by going on to hypothesis and experiment.

The novelist presents the material to be used in a reconstruction of the legal and conventional attitude toward the child, the woman, and the worker. He shows that the child is not merely a minor, but an individual full of impulsive imagination and eagerness. The realization that his nature is such leads the educator to try to understand it and adapt his methods to it, instead of roughly forcing the child to conform to set methods. Instead of forcing him to learn through fear of punishment or luring him to learn through hope of honor, he directs and broadens the child's own spontaneous interest. The new education begins with the novelist's appreciation of the child as an end in himself; it follows the intuition of the novelist that if we believe in life at all we must believe in the life of the child. The novelist also calls attention to the neglected personality of woman, of the worker, the criminal. He offers for aesthetic contemplation material which makes possible the reconsideration of institutions and conventions, and finally their remaking. Specifically he has drawn attention to the individual as the point of reconstruction. With this hint the social scientist is studying the individual, educating and emancipating him. If social change takes place through personal growth, understanding and guidance of the development of the individual should put the future of society in man's hand. The novelist himself does not go that far: he shows character in the very process of unfolding, and leaves it for reflection, but he thereby facilitates reflection. He is more than a reporter, for he can hardly help influencing the judgment of his readers. He stands by, observing the reconstruction of society, and at the same time helps it along.

In the words of Stuart P. Sherman: "Literature is a part and a tremendously important part of the environment of the mind. Its influence, though incalculable, is not in the slightest danger of being exaggerated. Its influence is immense. It is daily increasing. It is rapidly becoming the 'effective voice of the social government.' Just in proportion to its effectiveness as art, it takes possession of the emotions and thus controls the dynamic part of the mind."[8]

It behooves us, then, to consider how the novelist does make his work effective as art.

[8] "Unprintable," the *Atlantic Monthly* (July, 1923), Vol. CXXXII, No. 1.

X

THE TECHNIQUE OF THE NOVEL

We may say that the first English novel is Robinson Crusoe. It is very plain in form. Defoe merely enlarged upon a newspaper story, fusing fact with fiction and pretending to write a straightaway narrative of reality. It has the simple unity of one central figure. In *Clarissa Harlowe,* Richardson tried to give the illusion of reality by writing it in the form of letters, all bearing upon Clarissa, written by her, to her, or about her. Fielding also had one central figure, but had more sense of form, seeing the opportunity for the mock epic, writing massive digressive works treating man with over-solemnity. Smollett borrowed from the Spanish picaresque story, simply making the hero the reverse of a hero; but he is not in the tradition of the English novel, which, following the heroic epic, gives an evolution of character. It is only apparently formless in its variety and digressiveness, having the unity of life underneath.

Tolstoy, perhaps the greatest novelist, follows the epic. He is criticized by Mr. Lubbock in *The Craft of Fiction* because *War and Peace* has two parts: the cycle of youth and age, and of war and peace. But the two are related, since all the people are either in the war or connected with those who are in it; and the personal history is simply set off against the historical background. In *Anna Karenina* again there are two stories, but they are both on the one theme of marriage, and complement each other. In asserting that a novel should not contain two parts Mr. Lubbock is in sympathy with French literature. Whereas Tolstoy and most English novelists have felt that life does not present itself as a simple unit (in accord with the British philosophy of pluralism and empiricism), the French, on the contrary, have been monistic, their novels being lengthened short stories, exhibiting little development of character and brooking no digression, gaining in incisiveness but losing in scope, giving a single portrait where the English novel would give a group portrait. *Les Misérables* is of course an exception, Marcel Proust's and Romain Rolland's great works still more so. And in England there has been some reaction against the long novel toward the restricted French type, as in the work of Stevenson, and more lately in that of Swinnerton, whose *Nocturne* is concentrated within a few hours. Galsworthy and Wells, however, have tried going back to the long form. Some of the Russians have written short novels under French influence, but not Tolstoy and Dostoievsky. The Italians have usually written novelettes rather than novels, though *I Promessi Sposi* of Manzoni is long and leisurely enough. D'Annunzio writes the subjective inverted type of novel expressive of modern self-consciousness. The Spanish novel, as represented by Galdós, Ibáñez, and Concha Espina, is well unified about one or two central characters.

In *The Craft of Fiction*, by Percy Lubbock, two novel-forms are distinguished: the scenic or dramatic, in which the story acts itself out before the reader much as a play does; and the pictorial or panoramic, in which the author tells the reader about the story as he goes along.[1] The former is vivid, but limited in time and space; the latter is less vivid, but more free. Scene is best used to punctuate important points, especially the climax. The undramatic form of picture is best used for preparation, for information, and generalization. There is bound to be more or less of this in the novel and it is likely to be the dull part. The technique of the novel is therefore directed toward making this part, the pictorial, dramatic.

Mr. Lubbock's theory may be illustrated from the work of Joseph Conrad, because in the work of this one man we may find illustrations of nearly all the ways to write a novel. The ordinary method has been that of the omniscient author who constantly intrudes upon the story to tell the reader what he needs to know. The artificiality of this procedure tends to destroy the story's illusion, and unless the author be exceedingly interesting in his own person his intrusion is unwelcome. In his first novel, *Almayer's Folly,* Conrad was the omniscient author. As far as the story is told from the angle of Almayer the reader gets a consistent impression, and it seems as if Conrad had somehow got the tale from Almayer. But when the point of view is needlessly shifted to the thoughts of Almayer's Malay wife and other characters, the unified effect is lost, the illusion of reality is impaired. The reader begins to wonder if all these people had told Conrad their secrets. That being

[1] In Book III of *The Republic* Plato characterizes these same forms in criticizing the literary technique of Homer.

improbable, he must have made up the whole thing, and its authenticity is lost. The book surmounts this fault on account of its interesting material, the suspense introduced through shifting the time series, and because there is magic in it, the verve of a young man who was a genius enjoying the exciting adventure of writing his first novel.

The Nigger of the Narcissus may have no more historic truth than *Almayer's Folly;* yet it seems more true. This is not on account of Conrad's testimony, for, as Mr. Lubbock says, "The thing has to *look* true, and that is all. It is not made to look true by simple statement." *The Nigger* seems true because in writing it Conrad used the first device for rendering the pictorial form dramatic: he abandoned the method of the omniscient author for that of the personal narrator. This immediately makes a legitimate relation between the story-teller and his story, for he is himself now one of the characters in it; hence nothing he says can be an intrusion. Far from being surprised that he should know about the other characters, the reader expects it of him as an eyewitness. In attending to him the reader never turns away from the story. Mr. Lubbock says of this autobiographical method: "The author must supply his view, but he might treat his view as though it were in its turn a piece of action. It *is* a piece of action, or of activity, when he calls up these old recollections; and why should not that effort be given the value of a sort of drama on its own account? It would then be like a play within a play; the outer framework at least, consisting of the reflective mind, would be immediately in front of the reader; and its relation to the thing framed, the projected vision, would explain itself."[2]

In contrast to *The Nigger of the Narcissus, Almayer's Folly* lacks unity because the generalized narrator is outside and there is no apparent reason why the different threads of the yarn should stick to him. Yet Almayer could not have told his own story because the reader needed knowledge he could not have given. The personal narrator does very well in *The Nigger of the Narcissus* where the subject is the hovering of death over the black man and the effect thereof upon the crew; there is nothing here that he cannot substantiate. But one of the characters may not narrate the story when the subject is in himself, there being too many things he cannot tell about himself, unless the story be romantic, in which case the first person adds to the romance, as in *Harry Richmond,* by George Meredith. If the center of the story is outside the character who relates it, as in *David Copperfield,* the method of the personal narrator is legitimate. (Cf. *The Craft of Fiction,* pp. 128–31.)

Rather than have the chief character analyze himself it is better to enable the reader to see into his mind. To accomplish this the novelist abandons the first person and goes back to the third, with the difference that he now looks through the character's own eyes, yet without identifying himself with the character. If the important points in a novel fall within the mind of the hero the curtain must be raised even there and that

[2] *The Craft of Fiction,* p. 124.

inner drama revealed. The reader will still look upon the scene which the character sees, but instead of listening to his account of it he will regard it for himself. Mr. Lubbock explains: "It is still the man in the book who sees and judges and reflects; all the picture of life is still rendered in the hero's terms. But the difference is that instead of receiving his report we now see him in the act of judging and reflecting; his consciousness, no longer a matter of hearsay, a matter for which we must take his word, is now before us in its original agitation. Here is a spectacle for the reader, with no obtrusive interpreter, no transmitter of light, no conductor of meaning. This man's interior life is cast into the world of independent, rounded objects; it is given room to show itself; it appears; it *acts*. A distinction is made between the scene which the man surveys and the energy within him which converts it all into the stuff of his own being. The scene, as much as ever, is watched through his eyes; but now there is this other fact, in front of the scene, actually under the hand of the reader. To this fact the value of drama has accrued."[3] This is the method of Dostoievsky's *Crime and Punishment,* wherein we sit in the theater of Raskolnikov's mind. No other means could render that hidden terror. A generalized omniscient narrator would not be convincing, and Raskolnikov could not himself tell it afterward without weakening it.

When the interest is centered in the hero himself it is his mind which must be dramatized. Yet all the generalizing power of the pictorial method is retained

[3] *Ibid.,* p. 143.

because the panorama before the hero's eyes is seen by the reader at the same time that he is watching the drama of its effect within the hero's head. "Everything in the novel is now dramatically rendered, whether it is a page of dialogue or a page of description, because even in the page of description nobody is addressing us, nobody is reporting his impression to the reader. The impression is enacting itself in the endless series of images that play over the outspread expanse of the man's mind and memory."[4]

Conrad, however, could not have used this method for *The Nigger of the Narcissus* because the narrator in that book is nothing more than a unified apperception, an impersonal observer; if the spotlight of self-consciousness were turned upon his ego the reader would see nothing. To have made the narrator worth seeing in himself Conrad would have to have endowed him with a character, and that would have displaced the interest from the crew as a group, which is the proper focus in the story.

But in Conrad's *Lord Jim* there is a subject which might have been treated in the indirect manner we have been considering, for this novel is a story of psychology rather than of social psychology, like *The Nigger of the Narcissus*. The interest is centered in Lord Jim's soul; the adventure and the other characters are of no importance except as they set off Lord Jim. Conrad might have uncovered Jim's cerebration as Dostoievsky did Raskolnikov's, as James did Strether's in *The Ambassadors,* but he chose an approach more circuitous. There

[4] *Ibid.*, p. 170.

is no omniscient narrator; neither does Jim tell the whole tale himself; nor is his mind exposed to view. Conrad tells something in his own person; the understanding Marlow interprets Jim in a first-person narrative; Jim too tells what he can of himself; and others tell what they know until all available perspectives are filled in. In Conrad's *Chance* the story is again revealed from many angles, but the unfortunate Flora and her rescuer, Captain Anthony, are nearly obscured by their cloud of witnesses. In most of his work we see the effort to dramatize the parts which would naturally be undramatic.

In this Conrad was a disciple of Henry James, who tried to write at least one novel in which everything should be dramatic. In *The Awkward Age,* as Mr. Lubbock points out, he has foregone all the novelist's privilege of giving information about his characters, limiting himself to bare dialogue and action, with just a few stage directions, his advantage over the playwright being that he has insured a perfect interpretation of the lines by creating his own actors. It is doubtful, however, whether *The Awkward Age* could be given as a play just as it is, for, after all, the author's occasional comments are more than directions; they are necessary to the reader. This novel is a stunt which stands almost alone, because there is no reason why the novelist should deprive himself of the discursive value of panorama and picture, especially now that he knows how to dramatize these parts. *The Private Life of Helen of Troy,* by John Erskine, however, contains almost nothing but dialogue, and the talk is so good that it is sufficient; if descriptions of the palace at dawn or the garden at sunset had been inserted, the reader would certainly have been tempted to skip them. The setting is as simple as that of a Greek drama, so that a suggestion of it is enough, and the associations with Greek tragedy crowd in so thickly that the author is relieved of everything but the talk. It bears out Shaw's dictum that good conversation is what people crave. But then one may question whether these two books of Henry James and John Erskine are not plays rather than novels. A situation is presented, an interplay among well-defined characters; but not the slow unfolding of personality over a long stretch of time which is the essence of the novel. A novel in the true sense could hardly dispense with pictorial and panoramic passages.

In a novel which by nature is vivid these passages may be deliberately left undramatic to tone it down a little, lest it seem melodramatic. On the other hand these same parts may be manipulated to bolster up and authenticate violent drama, as in the work of Dickens. While picture and scene may be used to attenuate drama, they may also be used to thicken it, as in Balzac, where the careful preparation of the scene is wholly responsible for the power of the drama. In Conrad's *Typhoon* the description in the first fifty pages holds the reader back until he is ready to be launched upon a torrent of action.

It is noteworthy that while Conrad's subject matter is romantic, his technique is that of a realist, that he takes pains to authenticate his narratives. The first part of Scott's novels is like the slow approach of Balzac. But Dumas took no such pains. He plunged right into dialogue and action and kept it up, putting in explanatory material only when unavoidable. It may be said that the true romancer, like Dumas, has no technique, that he relies solely upon his inventiveness, fecundity, and zest in the story which gives him the vivacity of his style. The romancer has only to spin out his day-dreams to charm us. The realist is more occupied with technique because his is the harder task of interesting us in everyday people and places. He experiments with the effects of picture and drama, of indirect narration, in the endeavor to represent the values of our ordinary life. Romance forsakes familiarity and carries us to fairyland. Cabell has no use for literature which does not do this, and his constant effort, in which he splendidly succeeds, is to make us forget the real world. But a very great writer, like Tolstoy, inspires us to yearn for the soil and the hearth, to see romance in the homely things of life and love. A writer of his stature also brushes aside the intricacies of technique as cavalierly as the romancer. Thus Mr. Lubbock, aware of the greatness of Tolstoy, makes a bow to him in the beginning of *The Craft of Fiction* and then hurries by because he breaks all his rules of technique. Mr. Lubbock shows with good logic that picture and panorama should be used for the broad discursive sweep in a novel, but Tolstoy manages to cover immense areas of space and long intervals of time with nothing but drama and action.

Admitting, however, that the creative touch of genius evades analysis, the structure and form of a book is nevertheless instructive. To him who is aware of it the joy of reading is doubled, for behind his naïve pleasure in the story itself is his satisfaction in the skill with which it is told. By way of illustration let us take *Ethan Frome,* by Mrs. Wharton, who is often praised as the most careful craftsman among present American writers, and try to see wherein her craftsmanship consists. The setting is the cramped, sterile life on a worn-out New England farm in a terrible winter; the subject is the tragedy of Frome's love for his cranky, querulous wife's beautiful cousin who comes to help with the housework. The importance of the argument is heightened by the frame into which it is put, that is, by the first-person narration of the introduction and conclusion, which is sharply set off from the omniscient narration of the body of the story. The point of view is consistently that of Frome; his wife, Zeena, is always treated dramatically, never subjectively; and her cousin, Mattie Silver, is presented as a lovable girl, but never allowed to take the theme. This keeps the movement on an even keel and in itself makes *Ethan Frome* better than most fiction. Mrs. Wharton does not jump around like a crazy compass. The scope is limited to a very few characters and a small area. There is nothing panoramic about it. The description in the beginning is pictorial, and information is inserted in the course of it. Information required later is interpolated as reminiscence whenever a situation naturally suggests something in the past which the reader should know; it is never given chronologically, but always by association. The elements of personal description are few but repeated.

The beginning of *Ethan Frome,* then, is pictorial;

the rest is scenic and dramatic. Mrs. Wharton's first-person narrator, an engineer, is struck by the sight of Ethan Frome's broken figure; listens to the remarks of the stage driver, who knows only a little about him; notices the patent medicine he gets for his wife. Gradually he finds out more about the man; he discovers the severity of the winter; he learns that Mrs. Ned Hale knows more than the stage driver, but will not divulge it, which causes suspense; then he approaches Ethan himself, and the bleakness of the country is emphasized; finally he is taken into the doorway of the tragedy. This is the economical, gradual approach of the first twenty-eight pages, up to the point where the real story is slipped in by the omniscient author.

There is a temporal jump; the reader finds himself in the past, looking over Ethan's shoulder, sharing his feelings. Whenever the latter feels something that is not plain in itself the author inserts an explanation, as on page 29, about his having taken a technological course. His smash-up, first referred to on the second page, is constantly in the reader's mind, so that when Ethan stands outside the church on the coasting ground it seems that a sled may hit him any minute. While Ethan's point of view is kept all the time, there is skilful shifting to things outside it for the benefit of the reader. He sees with Ethan the dancing in the church, but he must know more here than he can gather by looking on, and so information is given him about some of the dancers: Eady, the son of the ambitious grocer; Mattie Silver, her coming to Frome's farm; his custom of escorting her home from parties, and his affection for her. For one paragraph on page 38 we join Frome in watching Mattie while we also see the effect of the sight within his mind. There is a sentence here serving like a close-up in a movie: "The face she lifted to her dancers was the same which, when she saw him, always looked like a window that has caught the sunset." Again we are permitted to see Frome's thought, this time upon his wife's dissatisfaction with Mattie's housework, and her hints that Mattie might marry Eady, with whom she is now dancing. Then our gaze is turned from Frome's mind to what he sees and hears: Mattie with Eady. Then when Mattie is alone outside the church we share his thoughts again. We see with him and within him. The talk about the danger of sleds colliding with the big elm sustains our anxiety about the smash-up. When the two get home there is a *scene*, the wife, Zeena, letting them in and standing looking at them with the unshaded lamp in her hand.

In the third chapter (p. 61) we have Frome's thoughts about Mattie in the morning, and the reasons for her coming to the farm are put in as though Frome were thinking about them. He thinks on for a page or so, and then, with the second sentence of the last paragraph on page 63, it seems to be the author who is informing about Mattie's home troubles and her coming to Starkfield. It seems to be the author, because if Frome were going over this matter he would hardly do it in the elaborate way in which it is presented, a man's own thoughts proceeding more by symbols and images, scraps of sentences. Still it may be Frome's own thought we are following, kindly translated by the author into grammatical form. At any rate it is plain that with the new paragraph on page 65 Frome is allowed to continue his own recapitulation of the situation: "Ethan alternately burned with the desire to see Mattie defy her and trembled with fear of the result." And: "Ethan . . . . could at least imagine that peace reigned in the house." Even here the author does not try to show us the actual symbols used in Frome's thought, but is careful to let us know that Frome is thinking, whereas in the preceding paragraph she passed her information directly to the reader without troubling to run it through him.

There is once more a scene with action (p. 66), when Zeena arranges her departure to see the doctor. A fuse is laid for trouble to be exploded later when Ethan imprudently tells her that the hired man will have to take her to the train because he must go collect cash for his lumber, something unprecedented. Then we are inside Ethan's head again (p. 72) while he contemplates the evening alone with Mattie, and reminisces about the illness of his mother and how Zeena came. We have external behavior (p. 79) with the conversation in which Ethan asks Hale, the builder, for advance payment. Yet the passage is only partially objective, the author giving lights on Hale and Frome. Ethan's thoughts are further exposed as he goes about other business in the village, returns home, and talks with Mattie.

The breaking of Zeena's pickle dish (p. 91), which she never allowed to be used, is dramatic in ominous portent. In chapter vii there is a scene when Zeena comes home, the author letting us see into Frome's mind meanwhile. In chapter viii the room is described which Ethan had made into a study; then he goes into it and thinks for the benefit of the reader. When Mattie finds him there next morning there is external action, though the reader still sees all the effects in Ethan's mind.

Our attention is turned full upon Ethan's thoughts when he plans to get money from Hale. Mrs. Hale's words of sympathy bring him up short when he realizes that he had been planning to take advantage of the Hales' sympathy to get money from them on false pretenses. He returns to the farm and external action continues parallel with his thoughts (p. 156).

At Shadow Pond the author tells of the picnic when Ethan and Mattie had sat there on a log. They recall this incident to each other, and overt behavior continues, with still a side-look into Ethan.

After the smash-up at the elm the reader finds himself absorbed in Ethan's returning consciousness.

Then comes the epilogue, in the first person, like the prologue. After the intense inner revelation of the story the "I" comes again with a jolt, for we had forgotten all about the first-person narrator. And yet this personal witness brings home the horror of the closing scene in the kitchen. "Frome stood hesitatingly before her as she advanced; then he looked at me and said: 'This is my wife, Mis' Frome.' After another interval he added, turning toward the figure in the armchair: 'And this is Miss Mattie Silver. . . . .'" This is a touch of superfluous irony, to make Zeena and Mattie exchange rôles, for Mattie is now shown querulous in the way that Ethan had disliked in Zeena. After the story has really closed there is further information from Mrs. Hale, which is excusable because we are glad to get it.

This story is remarkable for its economy and the carefulness throughout of its preparation for the catastrophe. It recalls Flaubert's *Madame Bovary,* which is taken as the fixed point in criticism of the technique of the novel. But, while it is interesting, technique is a trivial matter compared to the native genius of an author, his zest and gusto, sympathy, imagination and sheer creative power. That is what counts, the caliber of the author's personality. It is he who must animate the characters, the incidents, and the whole thing. The writer's personality is manifested above all through his style. Arthur Machen, in *The Hill of Dreams,* tries to discover the secret of style and confesses that there is in it a magic irreducible. In endeavoring to acquire it his hero took haunting passages from Poe, and by experimenting with them found that often the alteration of a single word would spoil the whole effect; but he also discovered that the strange splendor of *Don Quixote* was unimpaired by translation from the words of one language to those of another, as if it were independent of diction. All that can ultimately be said, then, is that style is part of the mystery of personality. Stevenson said: "Man is imperfect; yet, in his literature, he must express himself and his own views and preferences; for to do anything else is to do a far more perilous thing than to risk being immoral: it is to be sure of being untrue."[5]

[5] "The Morality of the Profession of Letters," printed in *The Writer's Art,* by Rollo Walter Brown.

With the recognition that his personality is what the author has to offer, the modern novelist seems to be dispensing with the technique of writing fiction, contenting himself with writing out his inner life as best he may. In *The Craft of Fiction,* Mr. Lubbock praises autobiography as a regular literary form, whose charm is in its fidelity to the winding course of the writer's thought as he muses upon the past. His own next work was of that sort, *Earlham,* which is a boy's memory overlaid with a man's. Plot, action, conversation are all laid aside as too crude to reveal the intimate self. Henry James was on the way to this, the only drama of interest to him being that of consciousness; yet even he had a balancing of parts, a conflict that resolved into a definite conclusion. But in the new novel the author frankly writes out his own personality for its own sake. The difference between the new subjective novel and ordinary autobiography is that in the former external events are unimportant, all that matters being the author's sensations and ideas.

It has been said that there is at least one novel in every man; now it is felt that there is only one novel in every novelist, the story of his life.

XI

THE NEW NOVEL

"The literature of the past is discordant with the vastness and variety, the reserves and resources and recuperations of life as we live it today. It is the expression of life under cruder and more rigid conditions than ours, lived by people who loved and hated more naïvely, aged sooner, and died younger than we do. Solitary persons and single events dominated them as they do not dominate us. We range wider, last longer, and escape more and more from intensity towards understanding."[1] A literature of the present is needed, expressing the actual reconstruction of society, and it is being supplied. The striking thing about it is its self-consciousness. Miss Rebecca West accounts for it thus.[2] In the Victorian age there were large families and small groups, whereas now there are small families and large groups, due to changed industrial and social conditions. In the Victorian age life was for the most part a family affair, whereas now people are forced "to live their own lives." It is obvious that a child who was one among ten children in a family, receiving one-tenth of the parental attention, would have a lesser notion of his own importance than the modern only child. Add to this that when the child of today goes out of the home he does

[1] Wells, *The Passionate Friends,* p. 359.

[2] Lecture before the Chicago Woman's Club, December 5, 1925.

not lodge in one small group or other, but finds himself up against a big impersonal world. The self-consciousness of his egocentric childhood is increased by the impersonality of the adult world which forces him back upon himself. Therefore it is no longer a rare person like Byron or Shelley who has a spiritual life of his own; the material of poetry has become the common stuff of prose.

Miss West says that if you told Thomas Hardy that you liked *Tess of the D'Urbervilles* or *Jude the Obscure* he replied with some disappointment, "Oh, but you ought to read my poetry; one can express things much better in poetry than in the novel." That is because the novel as it was when he stopped writing in that form, thirty years ago, was not suited to express the mood of poetry. A poet could write an ode at the peak of an emotion and omit what came before and after, but a novelist dealing with the family as a whole could not do that. He did not attempt to treat a character apart from his family. Even in sea stories, as in those of Marryat, the hero would start out from the family, each member of which was characterized, and would return in the end to that family, again described, with an account of what they had all been doing during his absence. The status of the Victorian did not belong to him as an individual, but was given him by his family or his station in the world. Thus, continues Miss West, the squire's coachman was an interesting character to the village because he was doing something unique; but a chauffeur in Chicago gets no individuality from his work, because it is just like that of a multitude of others. Occupation breaks down today as a principle of individuation, along with everything else external. George Eliot could write *Daniel Deronda,* about a Jew living in London; but today there are so many Jews in town that people do not think so readily of a Jew as a Jew, and as the peculiarity in his position diminishes he has to be treated like everyone else, as an individual.

It is the individual who counts now, not the member of a family, of a race, or any fixed group. The hero of the contemporary novel is not the figure whom others can see going about this or that business, but the inner being whom none can see but himself, dependent upon his self-consciousness for his existence, taking over gestures and ideas and whole rôles from others, but locking them in his own breast where he alone can pore over them and make them his very own, as a man studies the books of others until they are his. The individual goes abroad like a bird in search of strands of horsehair, bits of straw, and pieces of string, and returns to weave them into his nest. He turns round upon himself like a dog circling on a rug, knowing, like the dog, that the richest rug is not a lair for him until he has flattened down grass invisible to others and has shut his intangible self within a circle of his own imagining. It is this self, living in its own consciousness, which is the subject of the new novel, to which its form is adapted, a form often dispensing with plot and action, and even conversation, subjective, often sketchy and unfinished, but with the skill of Marcel Proust attaining to the utmost delicacy of analysis and expression, revealing the inmost chambers of the self, its intimate apparel, and the perfume of its very person. It is significant that the self-conscious Marcel Proust has nearly superseded the impersonal Flaubert as the French master of style.

Though there are sections of America which will continue for a time to produce the family novel, as in the work of Herbert Quick and Willa Cather, the center of literary interest is in the individual, in psychology, sometimes closely supported by observation and introspection, sometimes based on the extremest notions of psychoanalysis, as in D. H. Lawrence. This age is as adventurous in psychology as that of Zola was in biology, says Miss West. Everything is expected of it. Time was when people were naïvely judged by their acts, and novels were full of action; or people were thought capable of expressing themselves in conversation, and novels contained much dialogue. But now the belief is that the real self rarely shows in what one does or says, being buried in the subconscious. "It is no use trying to sum people up. One must follow hints, not exactly what is said, nor yet entirely what is done."[3] Consequently action is largely dispensed with in the new novel, and dialogue as well. It is in the past that the subconscious is revealed. The emphasis is not on the present, but on the past which it evokes, as in *The Judge,* by Rebecca West. Events are what past associations make them. In *The Judge* external events are depicted just enough to set thoughts going, and thoughts of the present always fade before the deeper thoughts of the past which they recall. As "every mother is a judge who sentences the

[3] Virginia Woolf, *Jacob's Room,* p. 46.

children for the sins of the father," every moment of life is sentenced by the years which begot it.

We live in the past. Significance flares up only in retrospect; then we look back and our present self is a pillar of salt which must be abandoned. Marcel Proust says that in present experience we merely expose the negative of the soul; we develop it afterward. The past is the only place where we can live, where we can find the self we seek. Conrad's brooding novels are an illustration. Something in the present stirs the mind, and the mind stirs the memory. Repeatedly in *The Rover*, for instance, an object is mentioned squarely in the present, but the sentence trails off and finishes in the past. For example: "Peyrol got up and opened his big sandalwood chest secured with an enormous padlock, part, too, of some old plunder gathered in a Chinese town in the Gulf of Tonkin, in company of certain Brothers of the Coast, who having boarded at night a Portuguese schooner and set her crew adrift in a boat, had taken a cruise on their own account, years and years and years ago." Again: "Cleaning the razor-blade (one of a set of twelve in a case) he had a vision of a brilliantly hazy ocean and an English Indiaman with her yards braced all ways, her canvas blowing loose above her blood-stained decks overrun by a lot of privateersmen and with the island of Ceylon swelling like a thin blue cloud on the far horizon."[4]

We are like old Peyrol, his lodging in a quiet farmhouse, his life in a romantic retrospect. Our self is not a bull's-eye under our coat, as some interpret Steven-

[4] Joseph Conrad, *The Rover*, pp. 36, 232.

son's *Lantern Bearers;* it is under the old coat we used to wear. We do not find our self in moral achievement, as Fichte found it, nor in artistic creation, as Schelling found it, nor in intellectual development, as Hegel found it, but in memory, which touches all that we do *after we have done it* with that peculiar "warmth and intimacy" which William James found to be the cachet of the self. In craving new experience to enrich our consciousness we look ahead to the self we will have in the past. A self in the future we can never reach; a self in the present we cannot hold. Expectation is for the past. When we look forward it is toward that which will have been.

Small families make people very conscious of their personalities from the beginning. Then they are chilled by the impersonality and indifference of the world, the Not-I, which makes them still more self-conscious, and self-solicitous. But what is a man's self save his past? In what shall he wrap it and protect it save in memories? A self is in the past because it is constituted by the rôles which *have been* taken over. When we ask who a man is, we wish to know who he *has been,* what he *has done.* If we learn that he is a lawyer, this means that he has been a lawyer. If he is a runner it is because he has been one. We are what we have been. There may be a shadow-line where a man is something before he has been it, but neither he nor others can be aware of it until it has been crossed. To develop a personality is to get possession of responses and habits which can be got only from experience, from a past. Our present need is always for a past. If there are but few situations which a baby can meet, it is because of the limitation of his experience.

When an old man becomes childish, it is due to his losing his past—"he is no longer what he used to be." A self is a past, and a man in full possession of himself is one in full possession of his past.

This is why novelists are coming to write more and more of their own personal experience. If the self is concealed from others in the present and lies buried in its past, showing in neither act nor word, then the only self which the novelist is privileged to know is his own. Formerly the characters in a novel represented classes and institutions. In the new novel there are few "characters," but there is always the individual. He is not placed by birth or occupation, for these are not the interesting things about him; all that matters is his self-consciousness. All authority and external restrictions of society are brought into the court of the individual's consciousness and questioned. The one question asked is whether in his sacred effort to be himself these other things help or hinder the individual, and without hesitation they are judged accordingly.

Galsworthy is interested in the democratization of law and property; Wells is concerned with the democratization of education; but they and all other contemporary novelists are chiefly occupied with the freedom of the love life. Politics and economics bear more remotely on the individual, though the present political and economic upheavals are threatening to make him more aware of them. But even when they annoy or frighten him he turns away whenever he can to the constant preoccupation of love. It is in love that he hopes to find the meaning of life and of himself. It is through love that he hopes to escape the narrowness of his past self and rise into the glorious self he would become. But here the novelist is sounding a warning. He says that love always disappoints the individual who expects too much from it. It takes him so far out of himself that he loses his way and is lost. In the end he is thrust back into himself and the contemplation of the past as the only reality he can be sure of. Yet he could not have a self resting on a past without having experience, and the novelist does say that the main thing in experience is love. But not merely the love of man for woman.

What really matters is the love of life, the faith of youth that life is passionate and poignant for all those who are sensitive to it, who can see and feel beneath the gray conventionalization that tends to overgrow it as one grows older. The novelist rebels with all the fire of the poet against growing up and settling down in a humdrum matter-of-fact world. Most people relinquish their dreams with adolescence. They put them aside with a sigh and become respectable citizens and taxpayers.

Anyhow, whether undergraduate or shop boy, man or woman, it must come as a shock about the age of twenty—the world of the elderly—thrown up in such black outline upon what we are; upon the reality; the moors and Byron; the sea and the lighthouse; . . . . upon the obstinate irrepressible conviction which makes youth so intolerably disagreeable—"I am what I am and intend to be it." . . . . Every time he lunches out on Sunday—at dinner parties and tea parties—there will be this same shock—horror—discomfort—then pleasure, for he draws into him at every step as he walks by the river such steady certainty, such reassurance from all sides, the trees bowing, the grey spires soft in the blue, voices blowing and seeming suspended in the air, the springy air of May.[5]

Youth, by Joseph Conrad, and *Prelude,* by Katherine Mansfield, throb with the assertion of youth that life is a tremendous adventure. Christopher Morley's *Thunder on the Left* shows how that "elderly world" settles upon the spirit of most people. Many become so thoroughly "grown up" that they do not know what they have lost, but very many are wistful and disappointed. Life is not as they had expected; they have not found what they sought. As Mrs. Woolf says in *Jacob's Room,* they turn millions of pages and turn from picture to picture in books and in life, looking, looking, for what? They can hardly admit to each other that they are questing after Romance and Beauty. It would sound quixotic. So they say little about it, but keep looking, in the newspaper, at the movies, at the theater, and in the novel. Some can find it all by themselves in solitude. They can write their own novels.

Were life adequately arranged there would not be this furtive seeking and day-dreaming. But as it is, the most interesting part of each one is kept to himself most of the time. No one thinks of saying what he thinks, except in occasional nocturnal confidences, under the spell of the sea or the stars. Yet it is no longer a very deep secret, this inner life of people, spread as it is on paper and screen. Perhaps in time reticence and isolation may be overcome. After all, the self is social. Why should it not be sociable?

[5] Virginia Woolf, *Jacob's Room,* p. 55.

This may be because while the self comes from association with others, it may be lost through too much contact. A certain amount of reserve is necessary to build up an individuality. The self would be dissipated if it overflowed on every shoulder. It must be slowly built up and saved up, protected in the presence of others by silence and small talk. La parole a été donnée à l'homme pour cacher sa pensée.

There is, however, a mean between extremes of the outer and inner life. This is most easily found in the modern city, which provides as much opportunity for seclusion as for society.[6] In rural communities a man has not been able to get away from people and their idea of what he is or should be. But in the city when he is off duty no one need know anything about him; he can live undisturbed the private life of his inner self. If he wishes he may be a philosopher.[7]

This is the mood of the new novel. Perhaps it is

[6] "Je vais chercher la solitude et la paix champêtre au seul lieu où elles existent en France, dans un quatrième étage, donnant sur les Champs-Elysées" (Stendhal, *Le Rouge et le Noir,* I, 228).

[7] Descartes wrote of his sojourn in Amsterdam: "However well appointed a country house may be, it always wants innumerable conveniences only to be found in towns, and the very solitude which one expects is never to be found there in its real perfection. . . . . Whereas in this great town where I now am, there being not a soul but myself who is not in business, everyone is so engrossed with his profits that I could live in it all my life without ever being seen by anyone. I go to walk every day amid the Babel of a great thoroughfare with as much liberty and repose as you could find in your garden-alleys; and I consider the men whom I see just as I should the trees which you meet in your forests or the animals which pasture there; the very sound of their bustle does not interrupt my reveries more than the murmuring of a stream" (quoted in J. P. Mahaffy's *Descartes,* pp. 50, 51).

only a mood, due to the forced individualism of city life and disappointment in material things and most social contacts. There is little opportunity for individual expression in work or play, standardized and machine-made as they are. The only place for it is well within the individual's own breast. If the whole city about him is as impersonal as a natural wilderness, like Descartes he must respond to it as he would to nature, personify and animate it with his own spirit, making its streets wonderful with the miracle of his own life.

The individual has to make life for himself when he is alone. Shut in his room he finds small comfort in the worlds about him, the impersonal worlds of industry, of science, and his nameless neighbors. He must seek solace in the world within. He must face life for himself and by himself, recognizing that people ordinarily meet only on the surface, that in love they meet deeper, but are ultimately forced back upon themselves. The new novel teaches that one is never less alone than when alone, that the self is lost in society and society found in the self. To have a self in the world the world must be in the self. The secret of life is social solitude. Thus, in *The Judge,* by Rebecca West, happiness is found in the intellect and in the appreciation of beauty; sorrow in human relationships, which are tangled and disappointing: "one still had to turn for comfort from persons to things." The heroine in Dorothy Richardson's *Revolving Lights* is typical of the new novel in prizing solitude above all, the silence in which things talk to her.

This point of view seems chilling and cheerless. One is moved to say that here art is lagging behind thought instead of leading it, for it looks as if novelists were just now giving emotional expression to the science and philosophy of the last century, which was mechanistic and analytic in the spirit of Descartes, breaking the world into bits of matter perpetually grinding against each other but never embracing or intimately intermingling. In that philosophy men themselves were part of mechanism, they were automata; or if they had souls these were locked up in their pineal glands, foreign to their own bodies and to the world wherein they moved. Each individual was involved in solipsism from which he could be extricated only by the help of God, which was cut off when science and philosophy destroyed the Cartesian proofs of God. Many recent novels seem to leave the individual in this sorry isolation, but there are indications that this is changing. Virginia Woolf, in *The Voyage Out,* says that the curse of modern life is our reticence and isolation. In the hands of many of the foremost writers the new novel is in accord with the most modern science and philosophy, which teach that the concept of organism is much more fruitful in explaining the world than that of mechanism.[8] Science now instructs us that synthesis is more important than analysis, that we do not understand our world when we reduce it to elements, for then we destroy it; and that there are no last elements, below them all being the sustaining, synthesizing force of life itself. The philosophy of evolution, joining hands with biology, teaches that instead of being cut off from each other and the world, each creature is essentially at one with

[8] Whitehead, *Science and the Modern World.*

all creation. And this sense of unity and harmony is the spirit of the new novel rightly understood. If surface contacts are still deprecated it is because they are felt to be slight and trivial compared to the underlying oneness of all being; which is quite different from saying that no real contact is possible.

The older forms of the novel are being abandoned, not in the interest of anarchy and formlessness, but from the conviction that life is so vitally, organically organized throughout all its manifestations that the effort to impose form upon it is a work of supererogation. The new novelist's faith is that if he sincerely express himself his work will have the inherent unity of consciousness, which is more coherent than a unity artificially imposed through any literary device. James Joyce has been most adventurous in this direction, and his *Ulysses* is a justification of faith in the solidarity of life. It is not the jumble it appears to those who have not the patience to read it. It hangs together despite the flouting of every fixed form of literary art. It holds together by its own inherent coherence. Joyce trusted life to unify his pages just as it unifies the hours of consciousness, without depending upon plot or artifice. Like life it simply emerges and grows, each event leading from another and to another, so that there is continuity throughout. Joyce does not teach that one must stay home by one's self to possess one's soul, as many novelists have done who were so jealous of the inner harmony of life that they feared to lose their rapport with it through external distraction. Joyce is more consistent in believing that nothing can interfere with it, that everything contributes to it. For him nothing is superficial or inconsequential. His attitude is sociable and convivial, like that of Marlowe and Shakespeare and the other great-hearted artists of the past, who were not afraid of life or love. He does not pretend that life is altogether lovely, but he believes it should be revealed and faced, even in its recesses of day-dream and reverie.

In the newspaper, on the screen, and in the novel the cover is taken off consciousness and we see into the secret places of the heart. Mr. Mead says:

> I wish to refer again to this inchoate phenomenon of the human reverie, which the press and the movie have projected before us. We are apt to consider it as a purely private affair with each individual, his desultory meanderings of idea and purpose and imagery, perhaps more gruesomely presented in James Joyce's *Ulysses* than elsewhere in literature. It is, indeed infected with privacy and therefore subject to disintegration. But it passes into the universal meanings of common discourse and co-operative effort, and out of it arise the forms of universal beauty, the intuitions of the inventor, the hypotheses of the scientist, and the creations of the artist. It is that part of the inner life of man which cannot be given its implicated meaning because of the incompleteness of social organization. It marks man's isolation within society. We have decried its vulgarity when the daily press and the movie films have stripped off its privacy. It is better, however, to live with our problems than to ignore them.[9]

The first step toward dealing with a problem is to take the aesthetic attitude toward it, to contemplate the values involved in it; and the function of the novel in our society is to facilitate this attitude toward social problems. *Richard Kane Looks at Life,* by Irwin Ed-

[9] George H. Mead, "The Nature of Aesthetic Experience," *International Journal of Ethics,* Vol. XXXVI, No. 4 (July, 1926).

man, is typical of the contemporary novel, taking up one after the other the values in education, travel, business, morals, marriage, news, art, politics, and religion. No decision is reached, but all sides of these questions are presented in emotional terms so that reflection upon them is unavoidable. Of course there continues to be a flood of novels of mere romance or mystery, to divert and distract people from their difficulties; and there is a sea of trash dealing sentimentally with serious problems, repeating trite attitudes and poses toward them that are no help at all to intelligent people. But the novels which are really new neither try to divert us from the perplexities of life nor soothe us with stereotyped answers. They do not pretend that college and a trip to Europe solve the problem of education, that success in business is success in life, that marriage settles the question of love, or church that of religion. They accept a changing world with shifting standards and frankly ask what the signs of promise are, pointing out the dangers and the hope that appear on the horizon.

They show how the reconstruction of society goes on through change in the individual. Thus vast social significance accrues to the often introspective and subjective approach of the contemporary novelist. Marcel Proust centers his theme in himself, his memories, sensations, and ideas; but his self includes Paris and the quintessence of present civilization. Modern life is distilled in his pages; what we see and what we look for everywhere we find in him. To read him is to feel one's sensibilities and intellectual penetration so refined that the illusion of complete insight is produced; and at the same time to find about one a subtle world suited to the exercise of that insight. His work is a perfect answer to the problem of developing and expressing a sensitive and comprehensive self.

Still it is only one answer and it will not fit everyone's problem. Preference for a novelist is determined by one's character, which it in turn determines. People read what they like and come to like what they read, but perhaps no one is ever satisfied with any one writer, since personality consists in taking over new attitudes and blending them together. The reason some people write novels as well as read them is that they feel they have something to say which has never been written; they can no more be satisfied with reading all the authors than others with one author. Of the making of books there is no end, because to read them is to be impelled to write them. The aesthetic attitude one takes toward the happenings in a novel gets carried over into life. It comes over a man that the most casual occurrence or ordinary scene would be absorbing if skilfully presented in a novel; and from the moment that he realizes this, or whenever he remembers it, there can be nothing casual or ordinary in the world! Then it is impossible to keep it silently to himself; he must share it, and, arduous and overwhelming as the task appears, the only way to share it is through art, and the only art which is accessible to most people is literature, though it be the most difficult. He would pick up what he has seen and pass it on to his friends, as he would a novel he had read with delight, for it is a new novel which he has seen—greater than Tolstoy's or Dostoievsky's or

Proust's! But it has not been translated into English or into any other human tongue; it has never been written at all, and never will be written by any but himself, for this novel is his own, and, however painful the process, he must bring it into being or die in the effort. And yet, after it has been so produced, it may look quite commonplace to others, and even to himself. But this is not what he had intended; this is a failure. With a sigh he turns back to Life, and *there* is his novel, darker and fairer than ever, beyond the reach of words, demanding to be written!

INDEX

INDEX

[PRINTED IN U·S·A]